Teaching Speech and Drama in the Infant School

D1435064

Penny Whittam

Ward Lock Educational

ISBN 0 7062 3590 8 hardback
ISBN 0 7062 3591 6 paperback

First published 1977

Set in 11 on 12 point Plantin
and printed by Robert MacLehose and Company Limited, Glasgow
for Ward Lock Educational
116 Baker Street, London W1M 2BB
Made in Great Britain

Contents

For Eleanor Clare

Acknowledgments

The author and publishers would like to thank the following for permission to reproduce material in their copyright: A. and C. Black Limited 'Moppety-Moppit' by W. Kingdon-Ward, 'Rowing' by Clive Sansom from *Speech Rhymes* edited by Clive Sansom; 'Skipping' by Ruth Sansom, 'Walking' by Clive Sansom from *Rhythm Rhymes* edited by Ruth Sansom; 'Kan-Kan-Kangaroo' from *Speech and Communication in the Primary School* by Clive Sansom. Jonathan Cape Limited and the Estate of Robert Frost 'Stopping by Woods on a Snowy Evening' from *The Poetry of Robert Frost* edited by Edward Connery. Evans Brothers Limited 'Splish-Splosh', 'The Grumpy Grandfather', 'The Two Rabbits', 'The Woodman', 'Windy Nights' from *The Play Way of Speech Training* by Rodney Bennett; 'Feet' by Irene Thompson from *The Book of a Thousand Poems*; 'Bonfire Night' by R. Brighton, 'Snowflakes' by J. Lambert, 'Train Talk' by H. Rostron from *Poems for Movement*. Samuel French Limited 'Donkey', 'Drummer Boys', 'Feathers', 'Snow', 'The Butcher's Shop' from *Junior Rhymes and Jingles* by Kathleen Rich. Ginn and Company Limited 'Uncle Vic' from *Sounds and Rhythm, Book 1* by Mavis Hampson; 'A Blanket', 'Bridges', 'My Glove', 'Slippers', 'What a Clatter' from *Sounds and Rhythm, Book 3* by Mavis Hampson. Heinemann Educational Books Limited 'Handy Spandy', 'Higgledy Piggledy', 'Just Like Me' from *The Merry-go-round* edited by James Reeves and published by Puffin. The Literary Trustees of Walter de la Mare and The Society of Authors as their representative 'The Huntsmen', 'Please to Remember' by Walter de la Mare. Macmillan London and Basingstoke 'Isn't It Cold!' from *Adventures into Poetry for the Primary School, Introductory Book* by Mary Daunt. Oxford University Press 'A hippity hippity hop', 'Criss-Cross', 'Dilly-dally', 'Sing Sing' from *Speech Training Rhymes and Jingles* by Hilda Haig-Brown and Zillah Walthew; 'Mick' from *The Blackbird in the*

Lilac by James Reeves. Pitman Publishing Limited 'Here Comes the Band', 'Jumping', 'Rush Hour', 'Swinging' from *We Play and Grow* by Maisie Cobby; 'Look Out!' from *Songs and Marching Tunes for Children* by Paul Edmonds. Ian Serraillier © 1963 'North-Easter'. The Society of Authors as the literary representative of the Estate of John Masefield 'Roadways' by John Masefield; The Society of Authors as the literary representative of the Estate of Rose Fyleman 'The Goblin' by Rose Fyleman. Mrs Iris Wise and Macmillan London and Basingstoke 'The Snare' from *Collected Poems* by James Stephens.

Illustrations: Hamish Hamilton Children's Books Limited *The Magician of Cracow* by Krystyna Turska. Hart-Davis Educational/ Granada Publishing Limited *One, Two, Three and Away Books* by Sheila McCullagh and Lois M. Myers. Hodder and Stoughton Children's Books *Marmaduke and the Lambs* by Elizabeth Chapman. Marshfields School, Peterborough *Skating* collage by children originally at Orchard Street School, reproduced as a Christmas card design by The National Society for Mentally Handicapped Children. Methuen Children's Books Limited *The Giant Alexander* by Frank Herrmann and George Him, illustrated by George Him.

Preface

Drama in infant schools will be at once a fulfilment and a preparation.

> A. F. Alington *Drama and Education*

This book is designed to help those teachers who wish to incorporate
drama, in its various aspects, into their work in the infant school. The
ideas contained in the book and the examples given have been tried
out by many teachers with whom I have had the privilege of working,
and where possible examples of the children's creative work have been
quoted. I should like to thank the teachers concerned for their
suggestions, for their willingness to test my ideas, and for freely
offering the results for inclusion in this book. The book is divided
into six chapters with a short comment before each, followed by the
ideas on that particular aspect of drama. However, there are no
divisions between the topics and these lead naturally into each other,
forming an integrated whole.

Some of the lessons are given in great detail. This is intended to
help the inexperienced teacher and to give her an initial confidence,
which in turn should make the children feel more secure. As the
teacher's confidence grows and she gets to know what her class can
do, she will be able to work more freely – adapting the structured
plan to meet the needs of her particular class.

Introduction

Drama and the infant school child

When we consider the characteristics and needs of the young child we discover that drama has a place in school, and that it can satisfy those needs in a variety of ways.

The young child is very active and he enjoys discovering his physical skills. He will therefore eagerly accept the challenge offered to him in a movement lesson involving actions he can carry out easily (which gives him confidence) and those that he has to strive for (satisfying the need to try out his skill). He begins by doing most of his work individually, in his own world, and then gradually learns to work with a partner and later in a group. This developing social sense is helped by the time spent in storymaking and improvisation which in turn satisfy his strong creative powers and the urge towards self-expression. Fantasy and reality are very closely linked and it is only gradually that the child learns to distinguish between them, though his need and love of fantasy never leave him.

His limited powers of self-expression will also be greatly encouraged, and with the opportunities for involving himself in speech and poetry (thus broadening his knowledge of language) his self-confidence will grow, he will have something to communicate and will be able to do so freely.

The young child has a passion for collecting and making things and will therefore enjoy creating large objects which can be used for drama, such as a pirate ship or a giant's castle. His inventive and adventurous spirit should not be stifled by the provision of beautiful ready-made costumes or props, and he should be given frequent opportunities to create his own environment in which something can happen. Drama is primarily a matter of activity and the child wants to be 'doing things' in his own way, although from time to time he needs and looks for guidance, reassurance and stimulus from his teacher.

The teacher's role

As in other subjects the teacher's attitude, her sensitive response to the children and her provision of creative ideas go a long way towards making a lesson successful. She should be ready to add to and enrich the children's own ideas, for as a child progresses he needs to be stimulated by fresh ideas which will in turn allow him to develop his imagination further. She should aim to create an atmosphere in which ideas will arise; where opportunities for individual initiative and independent thought and action go towards making the creative experience a satisfying one for the child. She must aim to achieve a balance between directed activity and free play. It should always be remembered that drama in education, more particularly with young children, has nothing to do with the highly sophisticated and technical achievements of drama in theatre. The intention is not to give a dramatic performance on stage with an audience, but to find enjoyment in *doing*, so that each child fulfils the potential of his own creative instincts.

Controlling the class

The teacher must set certain standards of behaviour and should not alter them from day to day. If a child is being difficult or upsetting the class the teacher could move and keep near to him; she could give him the responsibility of doing something particular and make it clear to the children in general that she will not have any of them spoiling a lesson for the others. With very shy children, in the early stages, encouragement to join in should be given, but without pressure. Let the child participate when he is ready. To children who are withdrawn drama offers the freedom of self-expression; to the already uninhibited child it gives opportunities to learn discipline and self-control; but all children have to learn to give and take within the group situation.

A practical way of controlling the class is to use a percussion instrument (e.g. drum or cymbal) so that the children learn to respond to the sound by being quiet and still. If it is used as a challenge they will respond, particularly if in the first few lessons they are given practice in getting accustomed to the sound, because very often when children are deeply involved in what they are doing they just do not hear it. Using a drum or a cymbal is less intrusive than when the teacher has to call out loudly. The teacher's voice is her principal weapon and her use of it is vitally important in creating and establishing the right atmosphere – loud, shrill or monotonous tones will prevent real communication between herself and the children. This in turn makes controlling the class much more difficult. This does not mean that a certain amount of noise is not permissible in a drama lesson – it is in fact necessary and will occur – but any furniture used should be lifted and not dragged; doors should be kept closed so that the sound of music or recording equipment does not interfere with the work of colleagues. Children who are not ready to use a large hall are frequently let loose in it, and as a result the teacher finds controlling and observing them virtually impossible. Space is of course needed for drama, but too often we forget what can first be done in the classroom, where themes and stories in which some children are static while others are moving can be specially selected. The same procedure can be adopted when first working in the hall. This can be followed by dividing the hall in half by forms with the children sitting around in a circle, semicircle or square, while activities take place within that shape; here the teacher can observe and control her group with a manageable space. Then the teacher can set up a larger space where blocks, levels etc. can be spread out for the children to use. It is important that the floor space is still the place where the main action occurs and the children should never be put up on stage.

1 Movement and mime

Movement is the basis of all work in drama. Akin to expressive movement is mime. It is not easy to say where one ends and the other begins. Perhaps it would be an approximation to truth to state that expressive movement describes ideas or experiences in abstract terms, whereas mime shows human experience in concrete terms, by representational movement. Mime is not mere imitation but needs to be genuinely imagined or experienced.

A. F. Alington   *Drama and Education*

In this chapter the ideas for movement and mime will be both a physical and an imaginative experience for the children and a preparation for drama activities.

Considerations when planning a lesson
Drama is concerned with the development of the whole child. Movement and mime have a part to play in this development. When planning the contents of a lesson various factors have to be borne in mind:

1 Movement should help towards the physical development and fitness of the child by giving him opportunities to discover how he can move the various parts of his body; to experience the contrasts of lightness and strength, to be able to move at various speeds and to feel the space he has around him. We aim gradually to make the child's body sensitive and flexible, a body which can work under control but without tension, a body in harmony with itself.
2 Movement and mime are concerned with the development of the

child's imagination, and when planning a lesson the creative ideas, themes or stories should be closely linked with the physical movements so that they prepare the children for the dramatic activities which follow.

3   Movement and mime are means by which dramatic activities are stimulated. But since children can only express what they have either experienced directly or through their imagination, the choice of ideas, themes and stories is very important.

Choice of themes

Children like and respond to the familiar things they see around them. In their play we will often see them rushing around being an aeroplane or driving a bus. They can switch very quickly from being a character to being an inanimate object.

Theme   THE STRANGE OBJECT
Aim

To enjoy working with absorption and control; to make good use of space and to give all children an equal chance to create.

Movement and mime activities
1   Moving as buses or cars, lorries or vans, fire engines etc.
2   Driving vehicles, steering to left and right.
3   Being the policeman directing the traffic.
4   Pushing, pulling, climbing up the 'strange object'.
5   Moving as (or in) the 'strange object'.

Musical instruments
Drum, woodblock, old bicycle bell, horn or hooter, spinning top.

Method of working
(*Have the children spaced out over the floor.*) Let's begin by running everywhere – off you go. Don't bump into anyone. (*Running beat on the woodblock.*) And rest. Let's see if you can sometimes run quickly and sometimes slowly. Ready. (*Woodblock – alternate quick then slow, then slow to quick and quick to slow gradually.*) Good. Now I'm going to use the drum. When you hear the drum you stand still. Off you go running – and listen out for the drum. . . . (*Big bang on drum.*) Everyone still? Run again. . . . (*Big bang on drum.*) Quite still. Listen. Run in and out of all the spaces you can find, in and out, but no bumping. (*Big bang on drum.*) And stop. Everyone come and sit by me. Sit down.

When you are coming to school in the morning what kind of things do you see going along the road? (Big lorries? Yes. Vans. Good, anything else? Buses. Cars. The milkman. Bicycles. A tractor.) If you heard a bell ringing what might that be? (A church bell? Yes. An ambulance. A police-car, oh, they have sirens do they, not bells? Anything else? A fire engine. Good.) So you might see all kinds of things moving along the street. You choose which one you are. You can be a big lorry, or a car, a bus or a van, an ambulance, a fire engine. Anything you like. Stand up. Ready. (*A mixture of instruments – ringing the bell or honking the horn now and then. If the children want to make their own motor engine sounds let them.*) And stop. This time you drive along the street. You choose what you are going to drive. Have you chosen? Now get hold of the wheel. Turn it one way. And the other way. Steer carefully one way. Now the other way. When you're driving you have to show which way you're turning, don't you? Put out one hand and show me which way you are turning. Good. What do you do if you want to go the other way? That's right. Now drivers, steer carefully and don't forget to signal clearly which way you are going. Here come the drivers. (*A mixture of instruments as before.*) And stop. Everyone drive to your own garage and stand still. Sometimes when we are walking down the street we see someone dressed in a special uniform standing in the road. Who is it? (Yes. The policeman.) What's he doing? (He's making the traffic stop and then go again.) How does he direct the traffic? (*Children wave arms.*) Show me what he does to stop the traffic. (*Children put their arms up in the air.*) Good. You be the policeman directing the traffic, telling the traffic to come on. Make good clear big signals. When I beat the drum you hold up your hand and stop the traffic. Ready policemen? (*Children wave arms. Beat on drum. Pause.*) Signal to the traffic again. (*Repeat sequence a few times adding helpful comments, praise and encouragement.*) And rest. Put your arms down. Let's work in two groups. Boys, you be the policemen and the girls will be the drivers. (*If preferred the teacher can divide the class by just pointing to one half and then the other half.*) Don't forget drivers, when the policeman puts up his hand saying stop you must stop. Policemen, make your signals really clear to the drivers and when you hear the drum beat you stop all the traffic. Are we all ready? (*A mixture of instruments then drum beat, pause, repeat sequence as required.*) Let's change over. Are you ready policemen? Are you ready drivers? Off you go. (*Instruments as before.*) And rest. Good. We didn't have any of the traffic bumping, did we? Come and sit by me.

Developing the theme

(*Children sit by teacher. She now tells story in her own words of how one day all the traffic stopped in a little town because there in the middle of the road was a very large strange object. No one knew what it was. It looked rather like a big stone but it did not feel like a stone. Everyone was very puzzled.*)

Let's imagine that our hall is the little town. You drive your bus or lorry, whatever you like, along the street. Suddenly we'll hear a big noise when all the traffic stops, and everyone sees the strange object in the road. So, quickly stand up. Have you chosen what you're going to drive? Off you go. (*A mixture of instruments as before.*) Listen out for the big noise when you stop. (*A quick sharp succession of sounds ending on a loud crescendo.*) Everyone still? (*The teacher, now by contrasting the loud noise with the quietness of her voice, helps the children to continue to work with absorption by introducing suspense in the atmosphere of the lesson.*) All the traffic stopped. There in the middle of the road was this huge strange object. This *thing*. The people walked around it, and they poked it and they knocked on it. What was it? You try and discover what the object is – poke it, knock on it – do what you like. (*Children react in various ways.*) Then the people decided to move it out of the way of the traffic. How could they move it? (Push it? Yes. Any other way? I've got a rope in my van, we can tie it round the thing and pull it – what a good idea!) Let's try pushing it first, shall we? Remember it is very, very large, so you'll have to push hard. (*Children begin to push.*) Push hard. Use your hands and arms strongly. That's it, bend your knees to help you. Try pushing with your shoulder sometimes . . . and rest. It was no use, the strange object wouldn't move. So let's use the rope. Tie your rope right round and then pull on the rope and see if you can make the strange object move. (*Children work at this. A slow drum beat could be used to give a rhythmic accompaniment, the teacher saying 'Pull,' 'Pull.' Some of the children may join in.*) Everyone rest. It was no use. The strange object would not move. Suddenly the fireman had an idea. He would climb up the object and look at the top part of it. What would the fireman have in his fire engine that he could use to climb up? (Yes. One of his big ladders.) Let me see you climbing up. Ready. (*A steady beat of the drum.*) Keep climbing until you get to the very top . . . and sit down where you are. When he got to the top he found a big hole and looking down he could see right inside the strange object. He was very excited. He called to the people and they all climbed up his ladder and looked through the hole into the strange object. Then one of them said, 'Let's go down into the *thing*.' So they all went down and sat in the *thing*. It was very quiet. Nobody said a word. Suddenly all the people heard a strange noise. (*The teacher can choose what she likes to make this sound. A child's spinning top could be used. As she works the top the children's attention will be focused on it.*) Listen to the sound. (*Let the top spin for a little while stopping it before it clatters over.*) Then, slowly, very slowly the strange *thing* rose up from the ground and went up into the air lifting the people up. Now you slowly, slowly rise up . . . rise up. Yes, you can lift your arms up if you want . . . and now float away. The strange object and the people floated away. . . . (*Quiet shake on the tambourine.*) Float, and sail and fly up into the sky and all over the town. (*Some of the children will be the strange object, others will choose to be in it.*) Sometimes, as the strange object went through the sky it bounced over the roof tops and chimney pots . . . (*quick shakes on the tambourine*) bouncing, bouncing, bouncing everywhere. . . . At long last it came back to the ground. So bring the strange *thing* back to rest on the ground. And everyone rest. Lie down where you are and listen. The people came out of the strange *thing* and went home. They no longer wanted to move the strange object. They were very proud of it even if they didn't know where it came from or what it was. They wanted to keep it in their town so that no one else would have it. And they all went to sleep. So close your eyes and have a little rest. (*The teacher should walk around and check that the children are relaxing.*) When morning came all the people woke up. Slowly, slowly, sit up. They all went out to look at the strange object but it wasn't there. They looked all over the town but they never found it and they never saw it again. I wonder what it was and where it came from and where it went to. (*The children could search for the thing but I think the quiet note to finish the lesson on is probably better.*)

Related activities for the classroom
1 Story writing. The older children could be encouraged to write about the *thing* – how it came to the village, what it was, where it went to.
2 Art and craft. The younger children could draw, paint or model their own version of the *thing*.
3 Build a large *thing* – see Chapter 3 for links with improvisation.

Some children are not ready to use the large space of a hall, and for others there is no hall to work in. So themes have to be found which enable activities to be carried out in the more confined space of a classroom.

Theme THE DANCING TREES

Aim

To give the children opportunities to work group by group, so making the organization easier in a classroom. They gain experience of discipline and control without losing the freedom to express themselves within the framework of the chosen movements.

Method of working

Prepare a space to work in by moving desks back. A possible arrangement is given below.

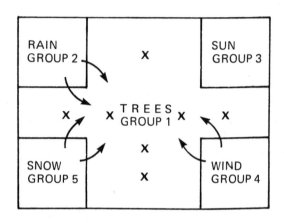

The trees are spaced out. The rain, snow, wind groups sit on the desks/tables until it is their turn to work among the trees. The sun group sits/stands on the desks/tables.

Musical instruments

The trees – tambourine
The rain – woodblock
The sun – drum
The wind – children make noises
The snow – xylophone

Movement and mime activities

Ideally all the children should have the opportunity to do all the movements given below, for example, while group 1 is moving in the central space making the rain fall, the others can do the hand movements for the rain while sitting in their places. It will take at least one lesson just to cover all the movement activities before finally dividing up into the five particular named groups for a story incorporating all the movements done by the children.

The lesson is taken in the same manner as the detailed lesson previously given, with the teacher using the various percussion instruments to accompany the different activities and thus controlling the class.

The trees (all movements can be done on the spot).
1 Growing from a small round seed into a big tree; various tree shapes; trees looking upwards towards the light and sun; tired trees with drooping branches heavy with snow.
2 Moving branches to feel and enjoy the warmth of the sun; bending branches blown by the wind; angry shaking branches to get rid of the snow.
3 Bending trees which fall to the ground.

The rain (opportunity to work group by group).
1 Using hands to make the rain fall lightly from high up in the sky to the ground.
2 In groups and making the rain fall.

The sun (the slow movements contrast with the quickness of the rain).
1 Experiment with a small group working closely together to make one sun, perhaps even with hands touching, spreading the magical warmth.
2 In groups moving and making the rain fall.

The wind (a further opportunity for the children to learn to move quickly without bumping into each other).
Work in turn, group by group, letting the children who are not moving free to make the sound of the wind. Moving and running freely using the whole body for the wind.

The snow (as they move the children are exploring the space immediately around them, and as they learn to work with control within this space there is less bumping).
Moving lightly, yet silently, making the snow fall with delicate, gentle fingers and hands – experiment with contrasts in slow falling snow and quicker falling snow.

Developing the theme
(*Before beginning see that the children are divided into five groups and arranged as in the diagram. Put the various musical instruments near the groups they accompany for ease of use. It is important that the teacher uses her voice sensitively by making a contrast between the narrative words and the words of help to the children.*)

(*Teacher stands by the tree group.*) Once upon a time there was a beautiful garden full of all kinds of trees. (*Tambourine – a quiet shake growing in intensity.*) Grow trees . . . grow . . . grow . . . grow. (*Children make different shaped trees.*)

(*Teacher moves to sun group.*) Each day the big yellow sun would rise up in the sky. (*Drum – slow roll, gradual crescendo.*) Slowly rise up, sun, slowly, slowly, spread your warmth everywhere. The trees liked the warmth of the sun – they lifted up their branches to feel the warmth of the sun spreading through their leaves. (*Children begin to move arms.*) Stretch your branches towards the sun, enjoy the lovely warmth of the sun. In the evening the sun would set, sinking down into the sky. (*Drum – a roll gradually dying away.*) Slowly, slowly, sink down and rest. (*Children finish by sitting.*)

(*Teacher moves to the rain group.*) Then the rain would begin to fall, first little drops of rain. (*Woodblock – quiet and quick. Children use their hands.*) Then the rain would fall all over the garden making all the trees wet. (*Woodblock quicker.*) Make the rain fall everywhere – all over the trees and garden. (*Children run in and out of trees.*) At long last the rain stopped and went away from the trees in the garden. (*Children return to their place.*) But then the wind began to blow very gently. (*Teacher to all the groups.*) Let me hear the sound of the wind blowing. (*Children make wind noises.*)

(*Teacher moves to the wind group.*) The wind grew stronger. Come on wind blow everywhere, blow on the branches, blow on the leaves. (*Children move in and out of trees.*) The trees in the garden were bending and tossing in the wind and there was a big storm. (*Tambourines shake.*) The wind blew fiercely and there was thunder and lightning. (*Teacher suddenly claps hands loudly and encourages the children to make the storm noises.*) The poor trees in the garden were frightened and tried to hide their branches from the storm. Slowly the storm began to go away. (*Teacher helps the children to lessen the sound by indicating with her hands.*) The wind left the trees in the garden and went away. (*Children return to their place.*) All was quiet and peaceful.

(*Teacher moves to the snow group.*) It was so quiet that the trees didn't hear the snow beginning to fall. (*Xylophone – very quiet.*) Make the snow fall just where you are sitting. (*Children use their hands.*) It fell quietly and gently covering the trees. Go and cover the trees with snow. (*Children move in and out of trees.*) Very quiet . . . very quiet. Cover the whole garden. The branches of the trees became heavier and heavier, the trees grew tired, the branches were so heavy they nearly touched the ground. (*Children respond by growing heavy and bending over.*) And then the snow went away leaving the trees all white. (*Children return to their place.*) The trees were cold and angry and shook themselves to get rid of the snow. (*Tambourine – quick and sharp.*) Shake yourselves, shake really hard, get rid of all the cold snow. The trees shook so hard that suddenly their roots came out of the ground and they jumped up in the air. (*Loud bang on tambourine. Teacher can encourage the other children to clap or play the instruments to accompany the moving, dancing trees. Tambourine – quick and excited.*) The trees moved and danced all over . . . they danced and danced till they all suddenly fell down with a great crash. (*Tambourine – loud bang. Teacher brings all to an end by indicating with her hands.*) Everyone listen. Because it was night time and there was snow on the ground no one saw or heard the trees. When morning came and the people came into the garden what did they see? (Yes. All the trees lying on the ground.) How would the people think the trees had got there? Why were the trees on the ground? (Because they had fallen over? They fell down in the storm. Yes. The trees had died.) The people would think of all kinds of reasons why the trees were lying on the ground wouldn't they? But they weren't right, were they? Only you and I know what really happened. (*To finish the lesson on a slightly comic note the teacher could wonder with the children whether trees could come out of the ground and dance.*) Wouldn't it be funny if we saw all the trees in our garden, or in the park, or outside school suddenly get up and dance about?

(This lesson can stand on its own or it can be used as preliminary work for the dramatized story of *The Selfish Giant* given in detail in Chapter 4.)

Related activities for the classroom
1   Using fabrics of different colours and textures the children could show the trees in three different scenes:
   (a)   trees in winter
   (b)   trees in summer
   (c)   trees in a storm.
2   A collection of various leaves could be made for the nature table.
3   Make and hang up a weather chart which the children take turns to mark up.

(N.B. The breakdown of the two lessons is only a guideline and teachers can adapt the words in the narrative and the words of help to suit the needs of their own class.)

Children like themes about the people they know and recognize. Among the early characters a young child sees – apart from his family – are the milkman, the postman, the baker, the dustman, the coalman and the rag and bone man.

Theme THE BAKER AND THE RUNAWAY BISCUITS
Aim
To introduce simple character work through occupational movement and mime and to link this with a short story. (*With infant children all character work is very broadly based since they are still being themselves; though in their play we see them enjoying role playing and imitating adults, e.g. their parents in the house, doctors and nurses giving medicine, shopkeepers selling etc.*) Themes of this kind also serve as an introduction to looking at other subjects, e.g. how letters travel about the country; the cow and what we get from milk.

Introduction
Discussion on the different kinds of bread, cakes and biscuits the children like to eat – sticky buns, sausage rolls, doughnuts, currant loaf, chocolate biscuits, etc.

Movement and mime activities
The baker
1 Walking slowly with bent knees carrying heavy sacks of flour
2 Stirring cake mixture round and round
3 Rolling out some dough
4 Driving the van and stopping to deliver bread
Shape-making
1 Growing into different shaped biscuits and moving about.
2 In pairs slowly growing into a big round bun and making up a funny bouncing dance.

Developing the theme comically
(*The teacher tells the story in her own words, filling it out by using the brief synopsis below.*)
The baker in the town drives around on Monday and Thursday delivering cakes and bread to the people. While the people eat their tea the baker returns to his shop. He stirs and rolls out the dough, cuts out his biscuits and puts them in the oven. Feeling very tired he goes to sleep. While he is sleeping the biscuits begin to grow until they are so big they have to open the oven doors and escape. They move through the town teasing the people by looking at them through the windows and then hiding. The people, so surprised, run and

wake up the baker by banging on the shop door. The baker does not believe them until he sees the biscuits looking at him through the shop window. He chases them in and out of the houses, the people watching. The scene ends with the biscuits climbing into the baker's van and driving off. The people all laugh and call out while the baker gives chase.

The setting

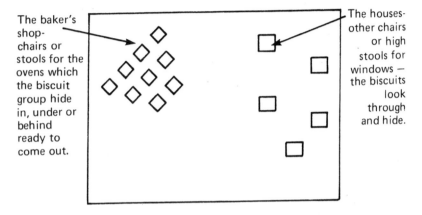

The baker's shop-chairs or stools for the ovens which the biscuit group hide in, under or behind ready to come out.

The houses-other chairs or high stools for windows — the biscuits look through and hide.

Percussion instruments
Used by the teacher to highlight the exciting points of the story:
Drum roll   – a quiet roll for the biscuits to grow.
Woodblock – quick beat for people when they knock on the door of the baker's shop.
Tambourine – for the chase.

Dividing into groups
Divide into three groups: bakers, biscuits and people. The teacher as narrator tells the story encouraging the children to speak. It does not matter that the children are speaking all together; in fact, it is easier for them and causes less self-consciousness than when only one child is made to be the baker.

Opportunities for speech work
1 The 'people' should be encouraged to think and speak clearly, telling the baker precisely what they want: 'I want six sticky buns please.'; 'What do you want today?'; 'Can I have a large brown loaf?'; 'How much is that?'
2 Ask the children what kind of things the people would say to the baker when they tell him about seeing the biscuits (and how he

reacts): 'I saw a big biscuit looking at me'; 'The biscuit made a funny face at me'; 'Don't be silly'; 'You must be dreaming'.

3 Encourage the children to make a noise and call out loudly and with excitement at the end of the scene: 'Come back!'; 'He's taken the van!'; 'Look, he's getting into the baker's van!'

Comment

It is with the use of speech that arises naturally out of a movement and mime theme that the link is made towards improvisation and dramatizing a story (see Chapters 3 and 4). Some themes do not call for speech, but the object of all movement and mime work with children is to enable them gradually to express their own ideas. Ultimately this means free expression through speech. So children should never be prevented from making sounds or speaking in a movement and mime lesson.

Other ideas on similar lines

THE POSTMAN (suitable for a hall or classroom)

Stage 1   *Introduction*

Introduce the theme through a poem which the children can quickly learn to speak; they can do the knocking action on the refrain lines and from this simple activity the whole theme can be expanded.

The Postman

Chorus	Rat-a-tat-tat, Rat-a-tat-tat!
	Rat-a-tat-tat, Tattoo!
Group 1	That's the way the Postman goes –
Chorus	Rat-a-tat-tat, Tattoo!
Group 2	Every morning at half-past eight
	You hear a bang at the garden gate,
Chorus	And Rat-a-tat-tat, Rat-a-tat-tat!
	Rat-a-tat-tat, Tattoo!

Clive Sansom

Stage 2   *Movement and mime*

The Postman

1 Knocking sharply and strongly for 4 beats and being silent for 4 beats.

2 Walking, stopping and knocking at the doors.

3 Bicycling – lying on back circling legs in the air; bicycling all around as the postman; bicycling, stopping, knocking and delivering letters and parcels.

4 Divide into two groups – one half the postmen, the other half the people opening their door to receive their mail when postmen knock.

Pillar-boxes
Growing into pillar-box shapes; half the class as pillar-boxes, the others as postmen carrying bags and collecting mail from the pillar-boxes in turn.

The village people
Running all over; half the class as people in village running and posting letters, the other half the pillar-boxes. (When class is divided always change over to give the children an equal chance to do everything.)

Stage 3   *Developing the theme*
(*First tell the story in your own words using the brief synopsis below as a guide.*)

One villager runs to post a letter. Suddenly he hears a ticking sound coming from the pillar-box. Very surprised, he listens, then runs and knocks on his neighbour's door. Neighbour opens it and is told the news. They both go to the pillar-box and listen. Continue story in this way until all the villagers are crowding round the pillar-box listening to the sound. They talk among themselves, asking each other what the sound can be. Some make suggestions: 'I wonder what it is?'; 'I think it's a bomb.'; 'I don't like the sound of it.'; 'Perhaps it will blow up!'; 'Can you see what it is?'; 'What shall we do?' etc. Just then the postman arrives to collect the mail and sees everyone. He says he will open the box. Everyone, rather frightened, runs and hides in their houses and peeps out to watch. As the postman goes to open it the pillar-box moves and jumps away from him. Postman runs to it but each time he tries to open it the pillar-box jumps away. Eventually he stops it and opens the door. Out comes a – (*children suggested the following ideas:* a kangaroo; a clock; a grasshopper; a frog; a letter-bomb; a rabbit; a watch; an elf; a wallaby).

Dividing the class
3 children make big round shape for pillar-box
3 children use woodblocks to make ticking sound
1 child as the postman
1 child to be hiding inside the pillar-box
The rest as the people in the village in their houses.

The setting

1   In the hall

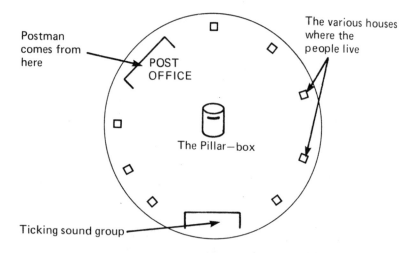

(The arrangement given, as in all the others, is only a suggestion. If working in the classroom where desks or tables cannot be moved then have pillar-box shape out in front and the village people waiting in their desks to be called. Children can knock on the desks and run from child to child using the gangways as streets.)

2   In the classroom

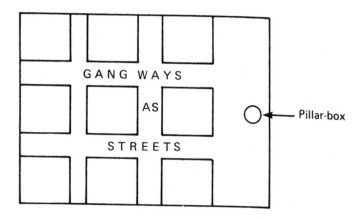

Related activities

1   Read from the poem 'Jackie Thimble' by James Reeves (in his

Complete Poems for Children published by Heinemann). It tells how Jackie, one day, climbed into a pillar-box and was shut in.

2 Tell the story of 'The Quacking Pillar-box' by Donald Bisset in *Time for a Story* (published by Puffin).

Stage 4 *An opportunity for an historical link*
(With the younger children stages 1–3 will be sufficient, but with the older ones a simple story on historical lines may be tried.)

Aim
To discover how our letters travelled about in the past and to show this in four short scenes.

The facts
In early times the only way a person could get a letter to someone who lived in another place was to ask a friend going there to take it. This friend most likely would be walking and it was dangerous because of the robbers in the forest. The only person who could use the post-horse was the king who had a group of special messengers. Later on there was a mail-coach which would stop in a town or village; a bell would be rung and the people would bring their letters to be put into bags. However, it was still dangerous because of the highwaymen who were always ready to hold up the coaches.

Movement and mime activities
1 A market with jugglers, dancing bears, acrobats, pedlars, lord of the manor etc.
2 Forest shapes; walking through the forest. Robbers creeping, hiding and waiting. King's messenger galloping.
3 Driving a coach. Walking about and ringing a bell.
4 Highwayman stalking through the forest.

Opportunities for speech
Talk about what 'Mary' might say to the king's messenger when asking him to take her letter and how he replies; then what 'Mary' might say to 'Joe' who is returning to his village.

What kind of things would the robbers say in scene 2 and the highwaymen in scene 4? etc.

A possible sequence
Teacher as narrator introduces story.
Scene 1: The fair
Everyone at the fair doing different things. The lord of the manor walking about watching. The king's messenger gallops in to deliver an important message to the lord. Mary asks him to take her letter.

King's messenger very proud, says he only carries letters to and from the king. Joe says he will take the letter.

Scene 2: The forest

The robbers camping, hear a sound and hide behind the trees. Joe comes along and the robbers spring out and try to rob him. Suddenly the king's messenger gallops into the forest and rescues Joe by scaring off the robbers. He says he will take Joe along with him on his horse.

Teacher says a few linking words before next scene.

Scene 3: The square

People all in their houses. Coach comes in with its two drivers; bell is rung and people come out and give their letters. Two other people climb into the coach and the coach leaves.

Scene 4: The forest

A highwayman gallops in and lies in waiting. The coach comes in and he holds it up: 'Stand and deliver!' Everyone has to empty pockets. Suddenly another highwayman arrives and the two quarrel; the first one drops the jewels he has stolen and the people quickly pick them up, climb into the coach and the drivers leave hurriedly.

Teacher makes a few concluding remarks, commenting on the contrast between the past and the present.

Comment

With this theme the progression from movement and mime into dramatizing a whole story can be traced. Other aspects of dramatizing a story are given fully in Chapter 4.

Other characters for consideration
The milkman
The policeman
The coalman
The shopkeeper
The garage mechanic
The farmer
The fireman
The bus driver
The roadmender
The dustman
The rag and bone man

A selection of twenty themes for lessons
At the bus station
The railway station

2 Storymaking

Every human being is born with imagination. . . . In terms of education, it is vital that each human being is helped both to develop his or her own imagination and to feel confidence in it. . . . To develop imagination there is need for constant opportunity to practise the use of one's own imaginative faculties.

B. Way   *Development through Drama*

One of the simplest ways of beginning drama with children is through the use of stories – stories which are created, sometimes entirely by the children themselves, sometimes with help from the teacher. These stories grow out of the children's imaginations when they are stimulated in a number of ways. In this chapter we shall see how by using sounds in various ways – rhymes; poems and songs; pictures and objects – we can help the children to make their own stories for drama.

THE USE OF SOUNDS

Using three percussion sounds

In the early stages of this work it is better to use just a few contrasting sounds for the children to respond to. The teacher provides the stimulus and allows the children to create freely. It does not matter if the ideas which come from them seem improbable or even fantastic. All the ideas should be accepted so that they gain confidence in their own creative ability. These ideas should be tried out by the whole class before the teacher selects some of them to put together into a story. The class should be given many opportunities to listen to contrasting sounds so that each story created should, in the beginning at least, be kept quite short. Young children can only sustain things for short lengths of time and the emphasis of the lesson should be on the action, on the doing which is drama, and not on long discussions.

Method of working
(*Have the children spaced out. Teacher stands in the midst of the group with a drum, woodblock and triangle near at hand.*)

Listen, what does this sound make you think of? (*She makes a strong, slow beat on the drum. The children will give a variety of suggestions.*) A giant? An angry bear, a soldier, an elephant – good. You choose who you are as you move about. Off you go. (*Repeat drum beat as children move.*) And rest. Now listen to this sound, what does it make you think of? (*Woodblock – galloping beat.*) A horse, knocking on a door, riding a horse, the rain falling – good. You do whatever you like while I make the sound. Ready. (*Repeat woodblock sound as children move about in various ways.*) And rest. Here's a different sound for you to listen to. (*Triangle – very quick, continuous beat.*) What's happening when you hear that sound? Father Christmas is coming, a fire engine is coming, it's a bell ringing – alright, you choose what's happening and when I make the sound I want to see all kinds of things happening. So choose what you are going to do. Ready. (*Repeat sound as children respond in their own particular way.*) Everyone rest. Let's see if we can put some of those ideas together and make a story. Once upon a time there was a giant who lived in a castle. He was fierce and strong. I will make the sound for the giant on the drum as you move about in your castle. Let me see how strong and fierce you are. Here come the giants. (*Drum beat as before with all the children being giants. Let them make noises for the giant if they want to.*) One day while the giant was in his castle a man came riding through the forest near the giant's castle, so climb onto your horse and off you go riding. (*Woodblock as before.*) The man grew very tired and seeing the castle he said to himself, 'I'll go and ask if I may rest for the night', so he pulled the long rope which rang the bell. He didn't know that a giant lived in the castle, so he pulled the rope and the bell jangled. (*Triangle as before.*) That's it! Pull hard and really make the bell ring. Now the giant heard the bell ringing so what do you think he did? (Got angry? ran to open the door. . . .) Good. The angry giant ran with big steps through his castle to the door. (*Drum – strong and quick.*) Run giants, really stretch your legs and see what big steps you can take. Yes, you can use your arms to help you if you want. What happened when he opened the door? He chased the man away . . . he stamped on him . . . the man jumped on his horse and rode away, the giant ate the man! Alright, you choose what your giant does, so get ready to open the big door slowly and carefully. (*Children begin to open door.*) Slowly, slowly open the big door – and now the giant sees the man. (*Drum beat – an excited roll followed by big bangs to act as contrasts to the controlled quietness of opening the door – sound grows to a climax and suddenly stops.*) Everyone rest and come and sit by me.

Comment
It will be noticed that the children's ideas are given at random and it is the teacher who uses them, puts them into a logical sequence to make a story. This means that the teacher must have the confidence to allow herself to accept all the ideas at first, and only at the end select some to put together. Once a teacher has tried this she and the children will find how exciting it is to see a story grow so naturally and spontaneously.

Other combinations of sound
1 A slow strong beat on the drum
   A quiet creeping beat on the woodblock
   Bells jangling.
   The children's final story (an example)
   The animals in the forest were troubled by a naughty bear and a stalking lion. Father Christmas comes and gives milk to the lion and honey to the bear. The lion lies down and goes to sleep while the bear happily dances and the other animals are troubled no more.

2 Drum roll
   Woodblock – slow and quiet
   Triangle – short sharp taps
   Tambourine – big bangs and jangles.
   The children's final story (an example)
   There is a big rock in the forest. A man creeps into the forest looking for the rock. He taps on it and the rock crumbles apart and golden treasure falls out.

An alternate method using three sounds
Working as before begin with the first sound (*e.g. slow beat on woodblock which could be for a slow stealthy creep*). Let the children do whatever they think of and then bring in the new sound by saying, 'What happens when he hears this sound?' or, 'What does he see when he hears this sound?' (*Each child is therefore linking his first idea*

directly with the next happening e.g. a big bang on the drum.) Then bring in the third sound by saying, 'What does he do when he hears this/sees this?' (*Quick beat on woodblock.*) Each child has now tried it out. The sequence could be repeated before the teacher, having talked with the class, decides on one story or a combination of stories for all of them to try out.

Developing the story

Having had experience of making these very simple short stories for drama, the children, however creative, will from time to time look to the teacher for further ideas and stimulus in order that their imaginations may be extended and the stories made longer. The teacher can now develop this storymaking further by seeing that they get what a child of any age always needs in a drama lesson, opportunities for individual and group work with:

1 plenty of action
2 happenings in various locales
3 simple conflicts arising out of the happenings
4 contrasts in atmosphere
5 different characters
6 good climaxes.

A sample lesson containing the above points is given below.

Theme   THE GOLDEN CLOCK
Method of working
(*The children come running/walking into the hall. Teacher stops them by a beat on the cymbal.*)

LOCALE	Everyone, quite still. Listen – let's imagine we are in a very grand palace and you are the proud king who lives in the palace.
CHARACTER	You like to walk about your palace wearing your splendid clothes. Think what kind of clothes you are wearing – perhaps you have a long cloak or a sword with jewels on it, maybe you are wearing your beautiful crown. You think of what you are wearing and how rich and proud you are. You be the king walking about now. (*Children become kings; teacher can give a slow beat on drum or cymbal. As the children move about, teacher says words of encouragement and praise.*) And rest. The king was very rich and had many beautiful

things in his palace but the thing he loved most was his golden clock. No matter where the king walked in his palace he could always hear the golden clock ticking. Listen to the clock ticking. (*Quiet ticking rhythm on woodblock.*) You walk as the king again and every now and then stop and listen, and make sure you can hear your golden clock ticking before you walk again. (*Drum and woodblock as before. Children are free to stop and listen when they want to. Teacher continues to help individual children by her words of comment, encouragement or praise.*) And rest. Now one

A NEW CHARACTER AND A CONTRAST IN ATMOSPHERE

day a wicked robber crept into the palace looking for the king's clock. He crept from room to room as he searched for the clock. You be the robber creeping and searching – remember to be very quiet because you don't want anyone to see you or hear you. (*Soft drum beat helps to keep the mood as children creep and search – the teacher has to feel how long the children can be absorbed in this, sustaining the atmosphere before she continues.*) Suddenly you see the clock (*Silence*) pick it

CLIMAX

up (*Children respond*) and run off with it. (*Quick excited beat on drum. Children run and some may hide.*)

CONFLICT

And rest. Everyone sit down. What do you think the king did when he discovered that someone had stolen his golden clock? (*Children give a variety of replies –* 'calls out the guard'; 'runs and looks everywhere'; 'calls his soldiers.') Good. The king was very angry

NEW CHARACTERS

and called for his soldiers who guarded the palace. What did he say to them? (*Children give various replies –* 'go and find my clock'; 'search for my golden clock'; 'find my clock or I'll cut off your heads!') So the king said, 'Find my golden clock, don't come back till you've found it or I'll cut off your heads!' The soldiers didn't wait a moment longer, they climbed on their horses and galloped off into the forest. (*Children begin to get up – ready to go.*) Climb on your horse . . . off you go into the forest. (*Galloping rhythm on woodblock.*) They rode through the forest looking everywhere for the robber. And rest. The soldiers got off their horses and went deep into the forest searching for the robber. Where would they look for him? ('under the bushes'; 'up in the trees'; 'behind the trees'.) Alright, you search under the bushes, look behind the trees and climb over the logs that are

VARIOUS
ACTIONS

lying in the forest. You may need to cut down some branches with your sword as you push your way through the forest. (*Children begin to search again. Teacher helps them to work with strength, pace and urgency by reminding them of the king's words. She brings the sequence to an end by a cymbal beat.*) Everyone sit down. The soldiers searched and searched but they couldn't find the robber or the king's golden clock. Soon it was night time and it became dark. The robber had crept into a cave in the forest with the golden clock. He was feeling very tired and the clock was very heavy to carry so he put it down in the cave beside him and went to sleep. The soldiers lay down in the forest, they didn't dare go back to the king. So lie down where you are. (*Children lie down and make*

A CONTRAST

themselves comfortable.) The soldiers were very tired. It was very quiet and still in the forest. They could hear no sound as they rested. (*Teacher lets children relax for as long as she thinks necessary before continuing.*) As the soldiers rested they heard a sound. It was very quiet and they listened hard. (*Very quiet ticking rhythm on woodblock.*) Suddenly they knew what it was. (*Some of the children jump up saying, 'It's the king's clock'.*) Yes it was the golden clock

CLIMAX

ticking – ticking loudly (*Ticking sound grows in volume until children finally find the clock*) to tell the soldiers

A CONTRAST
IN
ATMOSPHERE

where it was. The soldiers jumped up and ran through the forest. (*Children run in all directions.*) At long last the soldiers came to the cave where the clock was and they all suddenly stopped. (*Beat on cymbal.*) They crept very quietly low down near the ground (*Children respond*) towards the cave. And then they hid behind a big stone and watched and waited. And what do you think happened next?

Free choice to end of story

Teacher discusses with children various ends to the story. Children will offer a variety: 'The robber woke up and ran away'; 'No, the robber and the soldiers had a fight'; 'The soldiers took the clock while the robber was sleeping so he didn't hear them'; 'The soldiers captured the robber and took him back to the king'; 'The robber said sorry when he saw the king'; 'The king gave the soldiers a reward'.

The teacher decides on one end and the children try it out, working as before.

Group work

The children are now ready to work in groups and to try out the whole story with continuous action and sound and speech if they want it so that all the individual happenings with the different characters, changing atmospheres, surprise elements and good climaxes come together to make the story a creative experience for the children.

THE USE OF PICTURES

Illustrations, carefully chosen from various sources like children's books, magazines, newspapers, advertisements, old greetings cards etc. may be used to inspire a story which can be used for drama. Pictures which show clearly something happening and which contain one or two characters or groups of people are the best ones to begin with.

The picture

Aim

Not just to re-create what is happening in the picture, but to encourage the children to wonder what happened *before* and *after* the scene they are actually looking at.

Method of working

1   The teacher shows the picture to the children. Any printed words should be covered. The story is created by the children answering the following questions:

'Who can you see in the picture?'
'Why do you think he's an old man?'
'Why is the door nearly falling down?'
'Where has the cat come from?'
'Why do you think the cat is running?'
'Did the cat come in on his own or did the old man let him in?'
'What was the old man doing before?'
'What happened next?'

2   Drama activities out of the children's ideas.

(a)   Each child becomes the old man in his house, doing whatever work he wants, e.g. cooking, cleaning. Suddenly the man hears a noise (*Teacher can make a scratching noise for the children to react to*) and goes to open the door.

(b)   Each child becomes the cat moving about searching for a home; coming to the old man's house, miaowing and scratching on the door.

(c)   Divide into two groups. One makes the sound effects for the wind blowing while the other moves around as the wind.

(d)   Divide into four groups: the old man; the cat; the wind; sound effects. Discuss with the children the kind of things the old man would say to the cat and how the cat would answer. Then, with the teacher as narrator, the story could be improvised using movement, speech and sound effects. A possible sequence: the wind blows around the old man's house, he is busy in his room, the cat is frightened by the wind and searches for a home. Very tired and cold the cat arrives at the old man's door. Hearing the cat's sounds, he lets her in. The wind blows more angrily while he gives the cat milk and warms her by the fire.

Comment

Often the children want to be told the story in the book and the teacher could now read it to them showing all the illustrations.

Frequently this leads to the class wanting to improvise the whole story and in so doing they gain further experience in being new characters in fresh situations, and thus sustaining a longer story.

A variety of pictures

By our choice of picture we can give the children different dramatic experiences. For example, the two pictures on page 38 were chosen for the variety of characters and for the possibilities of group work.

Method of working
Similar questions, as before, were put to the children as they looked at the two pictures:

'What is happening?'
'Who are the different people you can see?'
'Where are the people?'
'What happened before the first picture?'
'What happened after it?'

What the children did (links with the dressing-up box ideas – see Chapter 3)

1   The children became the different characters in the park. They wanted to use the dressing-up box and having clothed themselves in various ways, went about doing a variety of things. Suddenly one of them fell into the pond and gradually they all helped to pull him out. The beginnings of group cooperation can be observed.
2   Spontaneous innovations followed because the children were creating happenings for themselves arising out of a true involvement in what they were doing. The physical part of the lesson which began with actions stimulated by the pictures, now became a creative experience.
    One of the boys threw another's hat into the water. The mother of the boy scolded him and speaking clearly and in character apologized for her badly-behaved son to the others. All the children responded in character to her and dialogue flowed freely between them.

Comment
This taking over of a theme or idea by the children will arise more often as they gain confidence and freedom in their work. The teacher must look out for these moments and handle them sensitively, allowing the children to create for as long as they can manage.

Fantasy pictures
The two pictures on page 41 offer the children opportunities to create fantasy stories where the elements of magic and strange happenings seem quite natural.

Pictures in a setting
The picture below links with one of the ideas in Chapter 3 – building an environment where something can happen. Here the children can build in the class or hall, using what furniture is available, a street with houses, shops, traffic and people travelling or moving about. The surprise element is the giant suddenly appearing.

Pictures with sounds
The lorry and the marching soldiers offer the children a chance to

use their percussion instruments in making the sounds to go with their story. (See *The use of sounds* on page 30.)

Seasonal and/or occupational pictures

These types of pictures, often seen in educational magazines, can be pulled out and mounted. They give the children varied opportunities in movement and mime activities which can be used in the improvising of a story. They are also useful to the teacher when introducing

a theme to the class to promote discussion, e.g. 'On the farm', and are particularly valuable with children whose resources and experience are limited, e.g. 'At the seaside', for those who have never visited a beach, or 'The railway station' for those who have never travelled on a train.

Written stories from pictures

The two stories below are examples of work written by the children after looking at the first picture (The old man and the cat) and the fourth picture (The giant).

1   *The old man and the cat* (Deborah, aged 6½)
Once upon a time there lived a man. called Mr fuss-pot. and his cat orlando. Mr fuss-pot. was a horrid man. he was selfish and he was mean and one day he banged his hand on the door. his hand went black and blue. and his cat bit him for being so noisey. Mr fuss-pot howled so loudly. that you could hear him throughout the town. he was so noisey. you would have heard him. if you were alive. now one day Orlando had a cold no one knew that orlando had cold so orlando died. and when Mr fuss-pot knew he was very very upset. and he told the whole town's people. and when they knew that orlando was "dead" they were very very upset. and so one man called Mr knibble sack gave Mr fuss-pot his cat. and now Mr fuss-pot lived happily ever after.

2   *The giant* (Mark, aged 6½)
Once upon a time a giant was in London he got there by rocket and he wanted to squash The people and he was in trouble because he couldnt go to The Shops or he would bash The Shops Down and he we dont no why he was in the middle of The road in London The giant Stopped and slowed The traffic down and The people were very angry and he didnt mind a bit and all The cars were bibbed The Hooters because he made a traffic jam and The cars made such a noise That The giant took off in his rocket and was never seen again

THE USE OF OBJECTS

Objects, real or imaginary, can be used as a stimulus for storymaking. This can be done in several ways:

1   The teacher creates her own story to tell the children; or the teacher and class together make up a story.

2   Storymaking by the class for improvisation.
3   Storytelling by the children individually.
4   As preliminary work for creative writing.

Using imaginary objects

One method is for the teacher to play a guessing game with the children, asking them to guess what is in her imaginary box which she unwraps and opens with a key, lifting out something carefully. By her handling of the object the class get a clue as to what it is. Then she encourages them to imagine they each have a box in front of them. They have to decide what is in their box. Working silently in mime and with concentration they are encouraged by the teacher to unwrap their box, open it and bring out what is inside. The teacher quietly asks some of them in turn what they have taken out, and then lets those who want to ask the others to guess what they have inside their box by the way they handle it.

Developing a story

1   The teacher and the children decide on an object together, e.g. an old map, a golden necklace, a whistle.
2   The object is then 'hidden'. The children decide where it should be hidden, e.g. in a tree trunk, under the floorboards, in a cave.
3   A story is gradually built up around the object by answering such questions as:
    Who hid it?
    Why was it hidden?
    Who found it?
    How did he find it?
    What did he do with it?
    What happened next?

An example of the children's story, using a map as the object

A map is hidden in an old tin can by two thieves called Bill and Pete. Two boys called Michael and Harry are playing on the beach and they find the tin can behind a rock. They look at the map. It is of the coast where they are and shows the caves. One cave is marked with a big cross. The two boys go to find the cave and search around. Inside they find a chest locked with big bolts. Harry has a penknife and they use it to open the chest. Inside they discover lots of beautiful jewels. Michael says it is the jewels they were talking about on the TV last night. They belong to the rich King of France's daughter. Michael says he will keep guard while Harry goes and phones the police. Harry goes off and Michael is left alone. Suddenly he hears a sound. The two thieves have come back. Bill is telling Pete how silly he was to hide the tin can so safely; now he can't find it. They search around. Then a torch light shines on them. There is great confusion as the thieves try to get away from the police who have arrived with Harry. The police take the two thieves to the police station and the next day the Princess arrives and gives Michael and Harry a big box of chocolates for finding her jewels.

Improvising the story
1 Activities for all the children to do
   The thieves – creeping across the beach, carrying the chest of jewels; hiding the map, etc.
   The boys – playing on the beach; finding the map; climbing over the rocks; searching in the cave; opening the chest.
   The policemen – walking about shining torches; marching off the thieves, etc.
2 Before dividing into groups, discuss how the thieves and the boys would talk to each other. What would they say? Would the thieves' voices be different from the boys'? Try out, in pairs, telephoning. What would the policemen say to the thieves and to the boys?
3 Group work
   Divide into groups of seven. All the groups working together in their own time. Some groups may only manage a very little dialogue; others will talk more freely. Each group has: 2 boys (Michael and Harry); 2 thieves (Bill and Pete); 2 policeman; 1 princess.

Stories written by the children
(a) Objects: A ship and a key
One day a rabbit was on a ship. The sailor had the key to the cage. The ship roked as the waves banged at it. The key was lost the next day. They looked all over the ship. it was no were. A day passed and at long last the rabbit found the key. the key was in the rabbit's food. The rabbit nibbled on the key.
(b) Objects and characters used together as a variation (A soldier, a lion and a bag)
The King of Spain wanted one of his soldiers to fight a lion who stole a bag of treasure. So the soldier galloped out of the castel and saw the lion. The fight began. the soldier fought well he killed the lion. He was the champion.

Using real objects

Another way to begin is to bring into class a collection of objects in a large bag. Let some of the children pick out the objects and by feeling them guess what they are. Alternatively, each child is asked to bring a secret object to school in a bag so that no one else knows what it is. Then in class the children swop objects and by touching them try again to guess what they are.

The teacher can create her own story to tell the children in which she uses objects as a visual aid, so that they are introduced to the idea of objects being brought into or forming part of the story. A brief outline of such a story is given below.

Objects needed: A toy cat; a ring

One night at Hallowe'en time two bad witches met and began to make up wicked spells as they stirred their big pot on the fire. (*Ask the children to make up a magic rhyme for the bad witches to say, for example:*

'*Ooka, Pooka, Widdleyum,*
Wincy, Bincy, Tiddleyum,
Wind spell, wind'.)

A little girl was lost and she suddenly saw the bad witches and heard them making up wicked spells. She was very frightened. Then she remembered the ring she wore on her finger which her grandmother had given her. She rubbed the ring (*the teacher now lets the children see the ring on her finger and rubs it*) and wished someone would come and help her. Suddenly, there in front of her was a big white cat. (*Teacher introduces the white toy cat she has sitting beside her.*) This was no ordinary cat, but a cat with magic powers. The little girl was so surprised, but the big white cat said, 'Miaow . . . what can I do to help you?' The little girl replied, 'Can you make a good spell which will break the bad witches' wicked spells?' 'It's very hard to do that,' said the white cat, 'but I will try.' (*Teacher asks children to make up a magic rhyme for the white cat, for example:*

'*Inca, Winca, Cinca, Linca,*
Inkey, Winkey, Wonkey, Wonka,
Un spell, Unwell.')

The white cat said the words, but nothing happened. 'We need help, can you ask some other children to say the words too?' asked the white cat. (*Teacher now asks the children listening to help by saying the magic rhyme.*) Suddenly there was a big flash of light and the bad witches disappeared leaving only their broomsticks behind. 'Climb up on the broomsticks with me,' said the white cat, 'and I'll take you home.' So the little girl and the white cat climbed on the broomsticks and flew up into the sky together.

(N.B. The story can, of course, be altered in a number of ways and be made as long or as short as required.)

Storytelling by the children

The teacher having told an 'objects' story to the children can now ask them to bring objects to their next lesson. Usually this results in the teacher's desk being covered with things from acorns to teddy bears and shoe boxes. The class will be eager to take it in turns to tell a story. Some of them will only speak a sentence or two; others will speak for much longer. Each child is therefore working at his own creative level. There is no pressure to do otherwise. A few of the children will only be able to talk about one or perhaps two objects, but many will be thrilled at trying to bring in as many as they can into the story. Children's imaginations are so free and where adults strive to put the objects together logically, the child will create without such inhibitions. Some teachers may be pleasantly surprised at the children's standard of storytelling, and how attentively the others will listen. Often this work will enable a child who has difficulty in writing a story of more than two lines to tell one quite freely. Gaining experience through practice of this kind will gradually help the child to think more imaginatively and thus write more freely.

Improvisation

Stage 1   *To tell an objects story*

The teacher can create a story which uses any number of objects, though to begin with it is probably simpler to use two, three or four. The various objects are put in a box and brought out, as a surprise element, as the story is told. The basis of such a story is given below. (It should be filled out imaginatively and told as a full story.)

Objects needed: a musical box; a little pottery jug; a corkscrew; a decorated bracelet – all put into a locked box.

Once upon a time a little boy called Bobbie had nothing to do; he'd played with all his toys and he couldn't go out because it was raining, so he climbed up the stairs and went into the attic. It was very dusty and there were lots of cobwebs about. Suddenly, in a corner, he found an old box with a key in it. (*Teacher unlocks the box and brings out objects to show the children at the appropriate moment in the story.*) He turned the key and opened the box. Inside he found a little wooden house with two people standing outside the door. 'I wonder what this key is for,' said Bobbie. He turned the key and listened. (*The class listen to the tune played by the musical box.*) Then Bobbie found a little jug and a pretty bracelet with a pattern all around it. At the bottom of the box he found an old corkscrew. 'If I use the corkscrew perhaps I'll be able to take out the cork in the little jug.' So he turned the corkscrew and out popped the cork. Smoke blew around him and there was a lovely smell and through the smoke he saw a strange man. 'I am the genie of the jug. What is your will, master?' Bobbie picked up the bracelet with the pattern all around it and said, 'Take me to the place where this bracelet comes from.' 'Come master, we must travel on my magic carpet,' said the genie, and they floated away to a far-off land called India. The genie took Bobbie to the market place and showed him the snake man. The man sat on the ground with a basket in front of him. He played a little pipe and as he played a snake rose up out of the basket and Bobbie saw a wonderful sight. The markings on the snake were the same as the ones on his bracelet. 'It is time to go home master,' said the genie, so once more Bobbie climbed onto the magic carpet and he and the genie floated all the way home. 'I'd like to see this house,' said Bobbie. (*Teacher holds up model of wooden Swiss chalet.*) 'Then we must travel on my magic carpet again,' said the genie, and together they floated away. (*Teacher winds up musical box and lets the music play as she speaks.*) They flew through the sky and the genie took Bobbie to a country of big mountains and snow. It was called Switzerland. On the mountain sides Bobbie could see lots of little wooden houses with sloping roofs. (*Music stops.*) Outside one of the houses he saw two people, a man and his wife. They were quarrelling. 'I don't want to go out in the snow,' the wife said. 'But I've got an umbrella for us,' said the man. 'It's too cold,' said his wife. 'But the snow won't fall on you,' said the man. He put up the umbrella and stepped into the deep snow. 'Come on,' he said, 'everyone will be waiting for us.' 'Alright,' said his wife. She stepped into the deep snow. But the umbrella covered her, so no snow could touch her. 'I'm feeling cold,' said Bobbie. 'Let's go back home.' So Bobbie and the genie returned on the magic carpet. 'It is time I returned to my jug, master,' said the genie. And before Bobbie could say another word, he disappeared. Then Bobbie rubbed his eyes and looked around him. There was his little wooden house with the two people standing outside the door. Had he really seen and heard them quarrelling? Here was the bracelet with the pattern on it. Was it like the pattern on the snake? And here was the little jug and the corkscrew. Did a genie really come out of the jug, or was it all just a wonderful dream?

48

Stage 2   *Preparing the improvisation*
1   Movement and mime activities can include:
    Working in pairs:
    (a)   Bobbie and the genie floating on the magic carpet.
    (b)   The snake man playing his pipe with the snake coming out of
          the basket swaying from side to side.
    Working in groups (let the children speak if they want to)
    (a)   Market scene: various activities other than the snake man,
          e.g. buying and selling, dancing animals.
    (b)   Winter scene: snow falling; people busy doing things, such
          as shovelling snow, riding in sledges.
2   Speech activities
    To help the children to use dialogue, recall the relevant parts of the
    story: 'What did the genie say to Bobbie when he came out of the
    jug?'; 'What did Bobbie ask him?'; 'Why were the man and woman
    quarrelling?'; 'What kind of things did they say to each other?'.
3   Percussion work
    The children should be encouraged to make their own music or
    sounds to go with the story. Let them experiment with percussion,
    e.g. sounds to go with the floating carpet; music for the snake
    man; sounds for the sledges moving, perhaps with bells jangling.

Stage 3   *Improvising the story*
Divide the class up accordingly:
    Bobbie
    Genie
    Snake man
    Snake
    Market people (each child in the group has his own special
        activity)
    Man
    Woman
    Swiss people (each child has his own activity)
    Percussion group
    Narrator – the teacher
Divide the classroom or hall into three areas: Bobbie's home; the
market place; in the mountain village – using forms, levels etc., but
keeping the whole presentation 'in the round'.

Comment
The method of work follows the same lines explored in the earlier
part of this chapter. The length of the improvisation will depend on

the children and this whole sequence of work, from the telling of the 'objects' story to the final improvisation, will cover a number of lessons.

THE USE OF RHYMES

Simple, well-known nursery rhymes can form a basis for storymaking. The children, using the situations given in the rhyme, develop their own stories for drama. They build up the stories by answering the questions put to them by the teacher.

Rhyme: 'Ride a cock horse'
Method of working

1   The teacher recites the rhyme to the children:

> Ride a cock horse to Banbury Cross,
> To see a fine lady upon a white horse,
> With rings on her fingers,
> And bells on her toes,
> She shall have music wherever she goes.

2   Now follows a discussion between teacher and children arising out of the following questions which extend the rhyme and so gradually build up a story:

> 'What was the lady doing?'
> 'Let's give her a name.'
> 'Who can remember the colour of her horse?'
> 'What shall we call the horse?'
> 'Can you remember where the lady was going?'
> 'Why was she going to Banbury Cross?'
> 'Why was she called a fine lady?'
> 'Do you think she really wore bells on her toes?'
> 'Who might she see or meet on her journey?'
> 'How could she have music as she travelled?'

3   The teacher now tells the story in its extended form, using the ideas she has been given by the children. At a certain point she can stop and offer them a new situation which brings in an element of surprise and excitement, e.g. '. . . and so Lady Esmeralda continued on her journey through the forest. Suddenly Joey, her white horse, stopped. "Come on, Joey," she said, "we don't want to be late for my wedding." But Joey wouldn't move. "What's wrong?" she said. . . . What do you think was wrong?' Had Joey hurt himself? Had he heard something which frightened

him? Why did he stop?' The class now offer various reasons and complete the story with the teacher.

4　Having made up their story the children are ready to improvise working along similar lines as in the previous section on story-making, e.g. all of them having the opportunity to try out all the characters and then dividing into groups to improvise the whole story.

An example of the children's story (given in brief)
Lady Esmeralda and a group of friends and musicians travel from her home through the country to Banbury Cross where she is going to be married. On the journey they meet various people, some of whom she is kind to. In the forest a group of robbers await her. Joey, the horse, stops because he's heard the robbers. The robbers, jump out and begin to steal all her presents and jewels. Joey runs off and brings back help. The people she was kind to chase off the robbers. Lady Esmeralda invites them to her wedding and they all go to Banbury Cross in a long procession.

Comment
The storymaking and then the improvising of the story would take a varied number of lessons depending on how much the children can create, and how long the story holds their interest. Sometimes an idea, particularly with the youngest ones, only lasts for a very short time. In other cases, if their imaginations are caught, it will be longer. Never prolong a theme beyond the needs of the children.

Other rhymes for storymaking
(Some need expanding less than others.)
A farmer went trotting upon his grey mare
The Queen of Hearts
Humpty Dumpty
Old King Cole
Little Boy Blue
Little Bo Peep
The house that Jack built
Old Mother Hubbard
Sing a song of sixpence
Simple Simon
There was a crooked man
Oh where, oh where has my little dog gone?
Pussy cat, pussy cat, where have you been?
Six little mice sat down to spin

Reading stories

At a time when most libraries, schools and families are having to cut down on the number of new books acquired, the Bullock Report *A Language for Life* (DES 1975) lays much stress on the importance of books in the life of a child. Reading stories to young children has been an integral part of the work in infant schools for many years, the children being introduced to a new world of fiction through seeing their teacher using and enjoying books. Their own appreciation of pictures and words is enhanced and the desire to read for themselves grows. I have, therefore, tried to give in the Appendix a selection of books which can be looked at, read and used as a source of material in the speech and drama class.

3   Improvisation

Improvisation is a term often used to describe school drama. It generally means acting on a given idea or theme without forethought or outside direction, and much of the drama in the Primary School should be of this kind.

J. Goodridge   *Drama in the Primary School*

Most of the ideas contained in Chapters 1 and 2 involved the children in creative dramatic activities arising from movement and story-making. In this chapter we shall consider various ways in which improvisation can take place.

One way is by building large structures in which the children can work and where things can happen – emphasis is on occupational activities.

Another way is by the use of costumes from the dressing-up box where the emphasis is on people and different characters.

Thirdly, using a combination of the first two ideas, environments can be created where people live and work.

In all cases the children are left free to play and exercise their imaginations, and the teacher observes what is happening. If themes or ideas seem to be emerging, she can, without imposing her own ideas, select one idea or theme for the children to develop. Often, after the time spent in free play, there comes a point when the children, unless especially creative and confident, look to the teacher for guidance and suggestions and it is then that she and the children begin to work out something together.

Since so much of this work is left free it is not possible to give ideas to try out in quite the same way as I have done in the previous chapters. However, I shall show below what happened with individual classes who tried out this method of improvisation. It may serve as a guideline to those teachers who wish to give their classes a chance to improvise.

Using the Wendy House

All children at some time or other use the Wendy House, or its equivalent, for play. It is generally used, in the early stages, for realistic play when routine, everyday, domestic activities take place, e.g. cleaning the house, washing clothes, cooking. At first each child tends to play in a world of his own but gradually becomes interested in what the others are doing. A small group may then 'play house' together, and sometimes the house becomes a shop, or a post office, or a hospital. It is now that the children begin to play at being characters and there is a mixture of reality and pretence in the play. For the purpose of improvisation the idea of the shop, post office or hospital can be extended to bring in the other children so that part, or all, of the classroom is converted into a hospital for example. They should be allowed to use any furniture, chairs, desks, boxes, and with help from the teacher they organize themselves. The classroom having been converted into a hospital the children are free to improvise. The teacher continues to observe, perhaps making discreet suggestions, but never trying to shape or polish the scene.

With one class who tried this it was evident that some of the children were acting out their fears about hospitals, and a useful discussion took place between them and the teacher who allayed fears and corrected false impressions. With this particular class the teacher went on to talk about Florence Nightingale and the children were eager to act out being soldiers lying in their beds (desks) with others as nurses scrubbing and cleaning the floor as ordered by Miss Nightingale. One child spontaneously became Miss Nightingale and walked up and down the rows between the beds carrying a candle and talking freely to the soldiers, comforting them.

It is interesting to note a link here between the imaginative, improvised work and the realistic playing out of the mother character who calms a child when he is frightened or upset. Far from becoming a bogey to them, the hospital idea helped these children to feel safe and secure.

Comment

In this kind of work the teacher, knowing the children in her class, has to judge when the time is right to suggest extending play to involve others. Gaining social experience through cooperation with others is a necessary part of the young child's growth towards maturity, and improvisation along the above lines gives the children the opportunity to work within a group situation.

Using large structures
Adventure playgrounds with their collections of large junk equipment provide a more continuous and changing source of pleasure to children than playing on more conventional objects like swings.

Children can be just as adventurous indoors, using old boxes to climb into, benches to walk across, tables to crawl under; and these objects often become the focus for simple imaginative activities, such as sailing away in an old rubber tyre. If a varied collection of large and small props can be made they can be used on their own or in conjunction with the furniture usually available in the classroom or hall. This enables the children to build large enough constructions or places for dramatic play.

Useful junk to collect
Apple boxes, cardboard cartons, an old plank, a log; some broom handles, tubs and barrels, large tins, ropes, old tools and gadgets, old sheets, baskets, lids, milk-bottle tops, centres from toilet rolls, an old wooden clothes-horse and an old tea-trolley.

How to begin
Some teachers who tried out this work found it easier to begin by dividing their class into perhaps three groups, each building its own structure, e.g. a ship, a bus, an aeroplane. Others found that their particular class built one structure which all the children used, such as a train.

Stage 1   Building the structure
The children were allowed to build their large vehicles in any way they wished, using what furniture and junk materials were at hand. Various activities followed as the children used their vehicles, e.g. some climbed into their aeroplane and became passengers, others preferred to be involved in flying the plane or steering the ship, some liked getting in and out of the bus.

Points teachers noted
1   Teachers commented on the real involvement of the children and the truth and reality of their actions, e.g. one girl warned another who was with her in the ship, 'Don't step over there, that's the the sea'; a boy had either observed someone or imagined himself

travelling in a train so accurately, that he stepped up into the carriage, having opened the imaginary door, sat down, read his newspaper, looked at his watch, took no notice of anyone except to ask the boy sitting in his carriage, 'Why isn't the train going?'

2   Some teachers were surprised at how good the children were at controlling and organizing themselves within their group, and how long they were able to concentrate and believe in the situation. ('I didn't have to teach anything, the children went on and on, they didn't seem to need me; they did all the work, I just watched. I suppose that was all right?')

Stage 2   *Dramatic happenings*

After the children had used their structures for a length of time, in some cases for one whole lesson, the teacher decided, by careful observation, when the time was right to extend the play. With some of the older groups the teacher needed to help in only a small way because the children were able to create happenings and stories very freely. But with the younger ones the teacher's help and guidance were looked for by questions such as:

'What could happen to make the train stop?'

'Can you think of something really exciting which could happen in the boat?'

'Shall we have a group of people travelling in the aeroplane?'

'Where is the bus taking all the people?'

In this way realistic play was transformed into an imaginative experience.

Points teachers noted

1   In the early weeks of the work the children's imaginative ideas were limited and simple:

One class decided that they were a circus company travelling on the train; suddenly one of the animals got loose and there was much activity as a search went on and then a great joint effort to get the animal back into the cage.

Another class which was working in three groups decided that at a given point, as if by magic, those in the ship would become different fish swimming in the sea; those on the bus would turn into various animals moving on the land, and those in the aeroplane would become birds flying in the sky.

2   Some teachers noted that having used various structures over a period of weeks the children wanted to keep one structure per-

manently – for example, the bus was kept by one class and used for the rest of term in conjunction with the Wendy House, which had been converted into a post office, and the shop, which was in another corner of the room. Each time the children wished to go shopping or to buy stamps or post a letter they travelled in their bus.

Stage 3 *Links with other classroom activities*

Arising out of the above point the class can be involved in the following activities:

1 Make tickets to be used on the bus.
2 Draw a map of the bus route.
3 Cut out some cardboard money to be used on the bus, at the post office and in the shop.
4 Look at real stamps and reproduce the correct colour and value on the ones made. Collect real used stamps.
5 Construct a posting-box which has a card showing the times of collection.
6 Use scales for weighing parcels and when buying food.
7 Letters to be written and the correct way to address a letter learnt.
8 Shopping lists may be kept and the price of foods entered.
9 All articles in the shop to be priced.
10 Each week different children can be the postman, the bus conductor, post office clerks and shopkeepers. At the end of the week the money in the post office and shop is counted.

Comment

With this kind of development, improvisation becomes part of the normal activities in the classroom. The experience gained in using speech helps the children to feel more confident and thus serves to bridge the gap between always doing everything in mime and the free use of dialogue when dramatizing their stories.

Developing a story using a large structure

Theme THE PIRATE SHIP
Introduction
With the children grouped around her, the teacher begins the story while the children close their eyes and listen and imagine. To help evoke the atmosphere and capture the children's interest, a recording of part of either *The New World Symphony* by Dvorak, or 'Four Sea

Interludes' from *Peter Grimes* by Britten, could be played quietly while the teacher speaks.

'One day, a long, long time ago, a strange ship came sailing across the sea. The sea was a deep blue colour . . . it was calm and the wind blew gently. The strange ship moved very quietly through the water . . . as if it didn't want anyone to know it was there . . . keep your eyes closed, can you see the colour of your ship and its big white sails? A group of men dressed in bright clothes were pulling on the ropes while a big strong man, with a black patch over one eye, was steering the silent ship towards a beach. From the tallest mast a flag was flying – a black flag with a skull and crossbones on it – can you guess what kind of ship this was and who these strange men were? (*Fade music out*) . . . Yes, you can open your eyes . . . that's right! It's a pirate ship with a whole gang of pirates on board.' (The handling of the end of the introduction will depend on whether the children guess correctly immediately or whether they will need more clues.)

Movement and mime activities

Percussion accompaniment could be provided by wire brushes on a drum giving the rhythm of the sea.

The captain

1 The children individually become the pirate captain and steer the ship.
2 Practise pulling on ropes to control the sails.

The ship

1 In pairs experiment with making the shape of the pirate ship – e.g. one partner holds his arms out in front for the prow of the ship, while the other holds on with one hand holding the other up in the air as the mast, or both arms are used to make the shape of the sail. Having worked out a shape they rock gently from side to side.
2 Let the older children experiment, in two groups, with making a bigger shape for the ship and incorporating the steering and rope pulling within the outline of the ship.

The pirates

1 Various occupational tasks on board ship – cleaning, sweeping, polishing, etc.
2 Leaving the ship by climbing into rowing boats; loading the boats with boxes of treasure, rowing ashore in pairs along the floor.
3 Pulling boats onto the beach, carrying or pushing or pulling boxes along a tunnel into a cave.

4 Dancing freely – stamping, clapping, waving swords, high jumps and low kicking jumps, slapping knees and kicking up heels.

5 Going to sleep in the cave.

Building the pirate ship

The introductory section and the movement and mime activities could be covered in the first lesson. In the second lesson the children can be left free to build their pirate ship using any furniture and junk materials available – boxes, broom handles, rope, old bicycle wheel, paper, milk-bottle tops, material for flags. Some of the children wanted to make the smaller props like the pirates' treasure – the gold and silver money to be put into bags and boxes; black patches to wear over their eyes. Once built the ship was ready to use in the next lesson.

Improvising the story

1 At the beginning of the next lesson, which was a double period, a new idea was suggested to the children from which they were to build their improvisation: namely, the cave on the beach into which the pirates went with their treasure was on an island where, unknown to the pirates, a group of islanders lived.

2 Discussion followed about the islanders and how they would feel and what they would do when they suddenly saw the pirate ship coming. Various ideas were put forward and used to make up a story.

3 The classroom was rearranged as the island and the class divided into two groups – the pirates and the islanders.

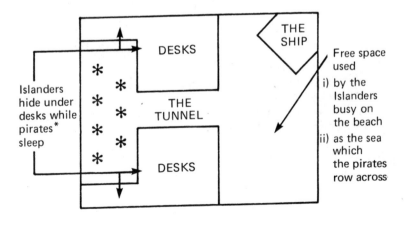

The story sequence given in brief

1 Islanders busy doing things on the beach. They see the ship coming. Frightened, they hide in the cave.
2 Pirates leave the ship, row across the sea carrying treasure and food. Find tunnel and creep into cave.
3 Islanders watch pirates from their hiding places.
4 Pirates eat, drink, dance, look at their treasure, go to sleep.
5 Islanders creep out and discuss what to do. A plan is chosen. All pick up stones and take them into cave.
6 Islanders replace treasure by stones. Take the treasure and row out to the pirate ship.
7 Pirates wake up, discover stones instead of their treasure. They run out and see islanders on their ship waving to them. Shout angrily 'come back'.
8 Islanders call out to pirates saying they are going to sail away and find another island.
9 The pirates dance about furiously.

Comment

The children who have been islanders will probably want to try being the pirates and *vice versa*. In improvisation of this kind it is easy for the children to change over since there is no problem with learning words and deciding who says what. The value of the experience lies in every child having an equal opportunity to use speech within the framework of the story.

Other structures to build
A bridge
A garage
A castle
A spaceship

Using the dressing-up box

It is only when a child sees creative possibilities in the clothes and materials in the dressing-up box that he will suddenly think of what he can do, who he can become, what is going to happen. Too often the articles in the box are complete, beautifully-made costumes like a fairy doll's dress or a cowboy outfit which, for the purpose of stimulating improvisation, are limited in their scope since the child who wears them can never be anything else but a fairy doll or a cowboy.

It is better, therefore, to have a collection of what may be described as 'indefinite' garments – garments which become what the child wants; garments which offer various possibilities.

Useful garments to collect

Lengths of material of different sizes, colours, texture and weight are the most useful. Old sheets can become tents, wigwams; net curtaining can be a bride's veil one moment, a tablecloth for a teashop the next; odd pieces of material can be used as cloaks, shawls, hoods. Often the texture or colour of the material will give the child an idea for a character, e.g. a striped oddment became an apron for a butcher, an old knitted scarf became a shawl for a gypsy.

Old clothes, such as dresses, skirts, jumpers, blouses of different styles and fabrics, can be used as a basis for most things – a dress for a queen or an outfit for a nurse. Old trousers, jackets or blazers can be converted into uniforms by the addition of bright buttons or a stripe down the leg. Stockings can be plaited and worn for hair in different styles. String vests dipped in a thin solution of paste and then sprayed with silver paint make effective armour.

Useful accessories to collect

Hats, bags, shoes, spectacle frames, belts etc. in a variety of styles are easy to collect and often it only needs one of these accessories to start a child thinking of who he is or what he is doing: for example, an old peaked cap is worn and the child is a workman in the road; a little evening bag is used to carry gold coins; a pair of old boots and a child looks for a sack to carry as Father Christmas.

How to begin

Stage I   *'Who are you?'*

1   Having collected together a variety of garments and accessories the children should be given the chance to use them freely, to experiment and to get used to putting things on without self-consciousness.

2   Group 1 is a *hat* group; Group 2 is a *shoe* group; Group 3 is a *costume* group which uses a prop as well; for example, a walking stick, a pair of glasses, a bag.

Each child in the group has been asked to bring one old accessory. (This is one way of adding to the dressing-up box.) Having put on his hat the child decides *who* he is and is free to do whatever he wishes as that person. The teacher and/or other children can play an informal guessing game of 'Who is the person in the hat?'; 'What sort of person is he?'

Similarly this can be done with Group 2 in a game of 'Who is the person wearing those shoes and where is he going?' and Group 3 with 'Who is he and what is he doing, carrying/using that bag (walking stick, glasses, etc.)?'

Stage 2 *'Where are you?'*
Having thus experimented with the free use of costume and gained experience in deciding on a character and an occupation from the use of accessories the children can choose to be whoever they wish within a setting where improvisation can occur; for example, *At the market.*

1 The teacher and children discuss what they know of markets, fairs or sales, such as a big city street or a weekly country market or a yearly local fund-raising sale with games to play and stalls like the white elephant.

2 The classroom is turned into the market.

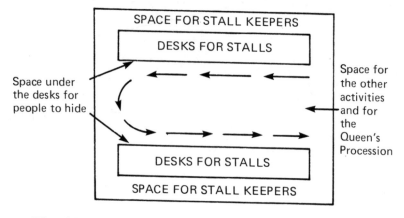

3 The children dressed in character improvise the activities in the market. (*At this stage it does not matter that individual children cannot be heard and that there seems to be no shape to the scene, but a lot of noise and bustle. If they are really concentrating then the apparent disorder is in fact an involved enjoyment by the children and has a purpose.*)

4 Gradually a simple shape can be given to the scene by asking the children questions like, 'What could happen to make everyone hide under the stalls?' (– 'a cow gets loose and the farmer chases the cow while everyone hides'); 'Can you think of someone very grand or famous who could come to the market?' (– 'the Queen could come'; 'the Mayor brings her to see the market'; 'someone

in the market gives her a present'); 'What prize shall we have for the lucky dip/raffle?' (*If tickets have been bought by the children then the moment when the draw is made by the teacher gives a natural climax or focal point to the scene, their attention being focused on one happening as in the previous examples.*)

Stage 3 *Improvising a story*
Theme   THE TOY SHOP
Introduction
A general discussion takes place about different kinds of toys. Then the children move about as the toys with percussion accompaniment:

rubber ball bouncing all over (soft sticks and drum)
toy steam train running (shakers)
teddy bear walking slowly (drum)
model aeroplane flying (tambourine)
an Action Man marching (woodblock), etc.

Development

1   The setting and a new character are introduced by the teacher asking the children, 'Can you think of a place where you can see all kinds of toys?' (– 'a toy shop'); 'Shall we have the toy-shopkeeper?' 'Is he young or old?' 'What does he do in the shop?' (The children become the shopkeeper busy in his shop, dusting, locking up cupboards, testing the clockwork toys, putting the toys away, counting his money, going to bed and hiding his money box in a safe place.)

2   The plot of the story is extended by the teacher saying to the children: 'One night while the shopkeeper was asleep someone very slowly opened a window, climbed in and crept about the shop looking for something – who was it? what was he looking for? how did he see in the dark shop?' (The children become a burglar climbing in, creeping about with a shining torch, search-ing for the money-box, finding it and beginning to leave the shop when the teacher who has been accompanying this with a very quiet stealthy woodblock sound suddenly brings it to a climax saying 'what happened?')

3   The idea for the climax to the story should come from the children ('the old man woke-up' 'he dropped the money-box and it made a loud noise' 'the toys chased the burglar'). One end is chosen and the children try it out, perhaps by dividing into two groups – one being the toys who chase the other group (the burglar) who drop the money-box and run away.

4   The end of the story is decided by the children, e.g. the toys put the money-box back and return to their cupboards or the clock strikes preventing them from doing this, so that when the old shopkeeper wakes up he finds his money gone, searches, finds it on the floor. Very surprised but happy, he dances about.

Using costume and props

The teacher divides up the class and each child uses the dressing-up box to dress himself as one of the characters in the story. While they are doing this the teacher can, if she wishes, sort out the instruments among the group who will help her to accompany the story. Props needed are a key, a money-box and a torch.

A setting in the hall

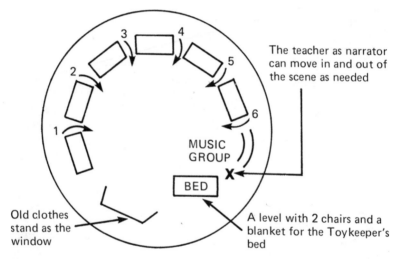

The teacher as narrator can move in and out of the scene as needed

MUSIC GROUP

BED

Old clothes stand as the window

A level with 2 chairs and a blanket for the Toykeeper's bed

Group key:
1 – Rubber balls
2 – Steam trains
3 – Teddy bears
4 – Aeroplanes
5 – Action Men

Music group does the clock striking and accompanies the story throughout.

▢ Levels placed upright on the floor. The toys stand or sit in the spaces between ready to come out (or toys can be groups on the levels).

A possible sequence (in brief)
(The teacher as the narrator opens and closes the story, and adds linking words during the improvisation if needed.)

1 Shopkeeper busy in shop with toys.
2 Clock strikes.
3 Shopkeeper puts away toys, locks up, counts his money and goes to bed. Silence.
4 Clock strikes and the toy groups in turn come to life and move about the shop.
5 Sudden noise. Toys all stop still where they are and watch.
6 Robber climbs in, creeps among the toys, searches, finds money-box. Begins to leave.
7 Suddenly stopped by toys who in turn call to each other and chase him around the shop. Robber drops money-box and leaves.
8 Clock strikes and toys return to their cupboards.
9 The old shopkeeper wakes up, finds his money-box gone and searches all over. At last he finds it. He is surprised and pleased and dances about.

Comment
If space is limited divide into a suitable number of groups and let each group have an old man, a burglar, a group of toys and decide on their own plot; then each group in turn shows their story to the others.

Other themes suitable for the use of costume
The circus
Hallowe'en time
At the zoo
A fancy dress party
In the street
Witches and wizards

Creating environments
Sometimes the use of costume can be linked directly with creating 'a place' physically where the children can improvise. If space is very limited these ideas are probably better tried out in the summer months when they can work out-of-doors. The method of working is as before.

Ideas in brief
1 At the seaside
Using furniture and junk materials the beach and sea area can be

marked out; rocks and caves arranged; fishing boat with nets is out at sea, while a lighthouse is at one end of the beach.

Activities include play on the beach and in the water, exploring caves, visiting the lighthouse, working in the boat etc.

Characters are those normally seen at the seaside – fishermen, children and parents, lighthouse-keeper, coastguard, donkey-man, ice-cream seller, creatures like crabs and seagulls.

Happenings could include a fishing boat returning late because of fog; the lighthouse shines its light, the people use foghorns and the boat is guided back safely. The children feed the seagulls and have fun in a Donkey Derby; the seagulls return to tell them a storm is coming so they pack up and leave before the big waves wash over everything.

2   In the woods

This need not be as elaborate as the seaside idea – a few chairs or posts could serve as trees, and upturned boxes could be logs for sitting on. A path could be chalked through the wood.

Activities can cover play or camping in the woods, tree felling, a picnic, collecting conkers etc.

Characters might be a group of villagers on a picnic, which allows the children a very wide choice; a group of tree cutters; animals like rabbits and birds.

A happening which may suggest ideas to the children is the sudden arrival of a stranger on horseback who, not realizing he is being watched, buries a box at the foot of a tree and gallops off. (See 'The Use of Objects' in Chapter 2 for links with this work.)

3   Other environments to create

In the farmyard
At the factory
The fairground
In the jungle
In the garden
On an island
Under the sea

Improvising a story

Theme   COWBOYS AND RED INDIANS
Introduction

A general discussion is used by the teacher to find out exactly what the children know about cowboys and Red Indians. A collection of pictures and objects can be made so that the children know what a wigwam, totem pole, tomahawks, lasso, cattle, tom-tom drums, ranch, round-up and canoes are. Some of the children may wish to bring articles from home, such as a cowboy hat, a feathered Indian hat and coloured Indian beads.

Using drums (or desk lids) let the children try sending messages by beating the drums in a rhythmic way:

(a) the cows are coming

the cows are coming

(b) Chief Big Hawk is sick

Doctor Doctor Doctor

(c) Cowboy prisoner

Cowboy prisoner

(Accents ∪ and – mark the light and heavy beats which are played on the drum.)

A cowboy song could be sung. Useful examples may be found in *Our Singing Country*, a book of American folk songs published by Macmillan.

Movement and mime activities

The Red Indians

1 Galloping on horses; galloping and jumping; wigwam shapes individually, in pairs, in threes; stalking by creeping silently through the forest and in and out of wigwams.
2 Paddling in a canoe.
3 Smoke movement by twisting and curling; totem poles with different shapes.
4 Dancing with high skips, moving round the totem poles, shuffling feet and bending body then lifting up hands to the sky, swinging tomahawks.

The cowboys

1 Walking in high boots by bending from side to side with each slow step.
2 Lassoes – swinging arms round and round, then throwing the lasso.
3 Galloping holding reins in one hand and the lasso in the other; riding a bucking bronco, then a weary horse.
4 The round-up – galloping in twisted lines to round up the cows.

5 The camp – lighting a fire, eating, resting then creeping in and out of the trees and rocks keeping a look-out.
6 Dancing by stamping feet, clapping hands, slapping knees, turning round, throwing hat into the air.

Building the setting

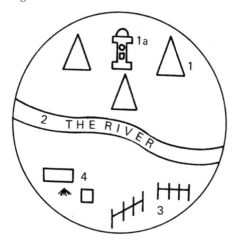

Key:
1 Wigwams can be made out of old sheets brightly painted by the children; three bamboo poles and some string will enable the wigwam to balance, leaving an opening for a child to be able to get in and out.
1a The totem pole can be built out of junk materials such as old cartons and egg boxes, and may be as tall as the children can manage.
2 The river need only be chalked out on the floor but wide enough to paddle in.
3 The ranch or stockade area may be enclosed by two old clothes-horses with a flag on a pole in the middle.
4 The camp could have a log, old boxes and a few sticks for the fire.

The story
One class used just the Red Indians for their story. Here is an outline of it.

While the girls were involved in cooking, washing clothes in the river, mending etc., the boys played in their canoes, built wigwams and laid a fire. Then one Red Indian said he was the strongest and should be the chief; he'd fight anyone. The chief was too old to fight so his son fought and lost. At night he left the village and rowed away down the river. Everyone was sad. The chief became very ill. No remedy seemed to make him better. The others told the fighter they must find the chief's son or he would die. And there was to be no more fighting. So they went in search. At last they found the chief's son. They told him about his sick father and the promise not to fight, and he agreed to return. The old chief was happy to see his son and he recovered from his illness. All the Red Indians celebrated by dancing and singing 'Land of the Silver Birch', a camp-fire song.

4 Dramatizing a story

It is true numerous plays and 'playlets' exist for use in the infant school, but most teachers would agree that 'ready-made' plays do not meet the needs of the children at this age . . . plays imposed upon the children are not real to them; they create situations which are entirely artificial. Moreover, the aim of providing opportunities for dramatic play in school is not to produce polished performances, but rather to promote the normal development of the children by encouraging them to express themselves naturally and freely.

L. McCrea *Stories to Play in the Infant School*

In the early stages of drama work the ideas we use need to be well within the children's knowledge and experience. We must start from the familiar. But gradually through the use of stories their knowledge of character and behaviour can be broadened and their imaginative horizons greatly extended.

For this chapter I have tried to collect a variety of stories for the class to interpret in its play-making. Although the stories have not been made up by the children, they are still encouraged to interpret them freely, to suggest variations in the plot and to use what dialogue they wish. Most will incorporate what they have heard in the story in their own dialogue but there is no pressure to memorize lines so there is variety at each playing which helps them to work spontaneously. A script is never written down. If the story is to be played before friends or parents some practice and rehearsal are of course needed, but the children should never be over-rehearsed. If they are, the result is the kind of mechanical playing in which spontaneity is lost.

Choice of material

Points to look for in a story:

1 A short story (long ones are too difficult to sustain) with a good, simple plot which has a clear beginning, a good development through direct action, but not too many incidents otherwise interest may be lost, and an end which satisfies the essential need the child feels for good triumphing over evil.

2 Characters should be real to the children whether they are human or animal. They tend to be of a broadly based type, e.g. a giant, a wicked goblin, an old man, which they find they can play more easily and with less self-consciousness than, for example, a character of their own age and background.

3 There is always some kind of conflict in a good story, and there must be a continuing interest in the fortunes of the characters – we wait with suspense to see what will happen next.

Setting the mood

As in other aspects of drama work the dramatization of a story is helped by an atmosphere of relaxation and freedom in which the children can respond to the story by the teacher.

Telling the story

The story should be told clearly and directly so that the class soon becomes familiar with it. Any complications in the plot which might confuse them should be sorted out and minor adaptations made before the story is told. Avoid telling the story too quickly but try to vary the pace by visualizing the happenings as imaginatively as possible. Try to keep the feeling of mystery or suspense, wonder or humour throughout and let this help in building up to a good climax.

Aims

Through this work the children should gain practice in thinking creatively and independently, in then learning how to work together and in gaining the confidence to express themselves through movement, mime and speech.

Sources

Fables and simple traditional tales

These stories with their simple repetitive quality, their animal characters endowed with human characteristics which children sympathize with, their simple dialogue, their plots where justice is invariably the outcome of the story so that no cunning or wicked character is ever so attractive as to win sympathy, and the good person is never made dull or ridiculous, appeal to all children. They are often the stories the children love to hear again and again and which they never tire of acting.

The story   THE WICKED GOBLINS
(Adapted from an old English traditional tale *The Hobyahs and Little Dog Tufty*. Versions of this tale can be found in *Folk Tales* by Leila Berg and *We Play and Grow* by M. Cobby.)
Arranging the classroom

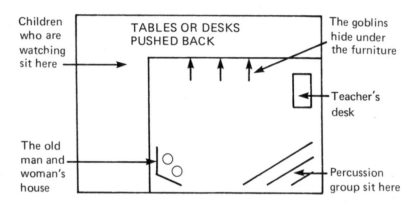

Using the limited space
1   Make what space you can with the furniture, e.g. the goblins can hide the old woman near the teacher's desk.
2   If only a few can work at a time encourage the other children who are watching to participate by making sounds, or playing percussion instruments so that they still feel involved.
3   It needs ingenuity to satisfy the needs of a large class when each child will want to play a certain part, but children do understand the fairness of taking turns and will cooperate if they know that their turn will come.

Preparing for a dramatization
(Children should be encouraged to interpret the characters in their own way.)
The characters (divide into three groups for ease of working):
1   The old man and old woman – moving about as the old man or woman doing various jobs in the house, then going to sleep by the fire etc.

2   Little dog Tufty – being the dog searching and sniffing out for the scent which leads him to the old woman etc.
    The goblins – growing into the shape of a nasty goblin; creeping about in the snow; creeping and hiding under the tables etc.
3

Speech and sound activities
1   Barking like the dog to frighten off the goblins.
2   Making strange noises for the goblins.
3   Saying the rhymes for the goblins:
    (a)   'We'll pull down the house
          We'll gobble up the old man
          We'll carry off the old woman.'
    (b)   'We've carried off the old woman
          Tonight we'll get the old man.'

Music making
Using percussion try out rhythms to accompany the story at certain moments, e.g. a slow stealthy beat for the creeping goblins.

Dialogue
Discuss with the children the things said in the story, reminding them through questions: 'What did the old man and woman say when Tufty barked and woke them up?' What did the old man say to Tufty when he found that the old woman had gone?' Encourage them to think of their own ideas ('What *else* could the old man say?') so that during the dramatization they feel free to speak, knowing they don't have to reproduce what was actually said in the story.

Dramatizing the story
(Divide the class into one group for the goblins, one group for percussion, individual children for the old man, old woman and Tufty; the rest to actively watch.)
(The teacher is the narrator and maintains the continuity of the story without imposing upon the children. She must time the telling in such a way as to allow the children the freedom to expand the scenes in their own way – extra dialogue or incidents may occur spontaneously and should not be stopped. It is through the use of her voice that the teacher helps the children to sustain the atmosphere and mood of the story.)
Once upon a time there was an old man and an old woman who lived in an old house with their dog Tufty. (*The three children can choose to do what they want – if various mimed occupational activities have been suggested and tried out during the preparation of the story they will have a variety of ideas to draw upon.*) One night while the old

73

man, the old woman and Tufty were sleeping some strange noises were heard. (*The group who is watching make noises and the goblin group come out, creep around speaking their threatening words* 'We'll pull down the house' *etc. The percussion group can accompany their stealthy creeping.*) Suddenly Tufty woke up. (*The barking noise frightens the goblins who run back to their hiding place. The old man and woman scold Tufty. The children will generally use different phrases at each telling of the story* – e.g. 'Stop barking!' 'What a nuisance you are!' 'We'll lock you up!' 'I won't give you any dinner.' 'Go to sleep.' (*They settle down to sleep again.*) All was quiet and peaceful. The old man and woman went to sleep. Tufty curled up in his basket. Outside the house it was very dark. Then quietly, very quietly the strange noises were heard again. (*Repeat as before.*) Tufty woke up again and barked and barked. (*Repeat as before, but this time the old couple lock Tufty in a cupboard* – 'Put him in the cupboard' 'Lock him up!' 'You're a naughty dog!' *Then they settle down once more.*) Once more it was quiet and peaceful. The old man and woman went to sleep. Poor Tufty was locked up in the cupboard, feeling very sad. . . . Suddenly the strange noises were heard again. (*Repeat as before.*) Tufty barked and barked but no one heard him. (*The goblins get into the house and take off the old woman and hide her. The old man hides when he sees them, while Tufty tries to get out of the cupboard.*) The wicked goblins hid the old woman under a tree and covered her up with an old sack. They ran back to their holes in the ground to go to sleep till morning. After a while the old man crept out of his hiding place and looked around. There was no sign of the old woman. Then the old man opened the cupboard door to let Tufty out. (*The old man talks to Tufty before the dog sets off on his search* – 'The old woman is gone, Tufty – can you find her?' 'The goblins have taken her away.' 'Search for her, Tufty.' *Tufty runs about sniffing; finds a scent, follows it to the tree and finds the old woman. She runs home and Tufty hides under the old sack.*) As soon as morning came the wicked goblins came out of their holes and crept around speaking very quietly and making strange noises. (*Repeat as before, using the second verse,* 'We've carried off the old woman, tonight we'll get the old man.' *The goblins move towards the sack.*) But this time Tufty was waiting for them and he jumped out! (*Tufty gives the goblins a great surprise* – *much noise follows including percussion sounds as he barks and chases them round and round until they finally go away.*) The goblins were so frightened that they ran away and never returned. Then Tufty went home. (*He is given a great welcome by the old couple. The children will have suggested various presents he could be given* – 'A big bone', 'lots of dog biscuits', 'a special dinner', 'a new basket', 'a new collar and lead'.) The old man and woman said Tufty was the cleverest and bravest dog in the world. And Tufty lived happily ever after with them.

Comment
The dramatization given above is one way of adapting the story; each teacher will choose her own words when telling the tale and often, having done the story, the children will enjoy suggesting other things that could happen. After this they might make up another adventure for little dog Tufty and the old couple.

Other examples
The Little Red Hen; Three Little Pigs; The Gingerbread Man – all in *The Three Bears and Fifteen Other Stories* by Anne Rockwell.
Dick Whittington; The Little Rabbits; Red Riding Hood – from 'Favourite Books' series (Nelson).
The Three Billy Goats Gruff; Chanticleer; Foolish Mr Grasshopper – from *We Play and Grow* by Maisie Cobby.
The Story of King Arthur; Robin Hood Goes to Market; St George and the Dragon – from *Stories to Play in the Infant School* by Lilian McCrea.

Fairy tales and folk tales
These stories, some famous, some less well known, are invaluable and should form part of every child's early experience. From the very openings of the stories all kinds of dramatic situations seem possible. The child's imagination is caught and held through a series of events, sometimes fantastic, which are not all necessarily happy. The child readily identifies with the characters whether the story shows the triumph of a good person over a bad one, as in *Snow-White*; proving oneself through heroic deeds, as in *Jack and the Beanstalk*; seeing the underdog win over everyone else, as in *The Golden Goose*; outwitting the wicked, as in *Hansel and Gretel*; showing how kindness is rewarded, as in *Beauty and the Beast*; and how the truth about a person is always discovered in the end, as in *The Princess and the Pea*.

Because they are set in the past, in distant lands where magic rules, and where animals talk and behave like humans, fairy tales allow the child's imagination to escape into a fantasy world where all things are possible and where all one's wishes can be fulfilled.

Folk tales, which are concerned more with ordinary people, appeal because they deal with matters of everyday life, such as overcoming obstacles in order to eat, as in *The Three Billy Goats Gruff*, and the need to survive, as in *Why the Robin has a Red Breast*. Often the tales have a humorous element, like the old man in the Russian tale who has to cope with the biggest turnip in the world, or the Emperor with his new clothes which do not really exist.

The Story THE FARMER AND THE TURNIP
(Versions of this story can be found in *The Old Man and The Turnip*, a Read-Aloud Book published by Collins and *My First Big Story Book*, a Young Puffin Book.)
Working in the hall or a large space
Before beginning the dramatization in the hall the children should have been told the story in the more intimate atmosphere of the classroom.

Once in the hall take the children through the whole story so that they have an opportunity to be all the characters. This will probably take up a whole lesson and is important in giving the children the foundation of experience needed before breaking up into groups. It also means that no child feels he is being left out or overlooked, and that there is no 'cast' as such – just different children being different characters at each telling of the story. The advantage of this aspect of drama work is that they can all play any of the characters; it is the whole class who tell the story.

Preparing for a dramatization
The various characters and incidents given are for the adaptation I have made. With fairy tales and folk tales various versions are available and the teacher can decide which she thinks will suit her class best or she can make her own adaptation of the tale.
The characters (speech to be encouraged):

1 The farmer working in his field – digging the soil, raking the earth, planting seeds etc.
2 The farmer's wife working in the house – cleaning, washing clothes, cooking, etc. (*So the whole class is actively engaged.*)
Divide into pairs so that each farmer has a wife, and let them speak together – perhaps the farmer's wife telling him about the mayor coming to the village so they decide to go and see him. Through discussion with the children other ideas will emerge about the kind of things they say to each other before they ride off together. (*At this point, since all the children are speaking, no individual child will be heard, but this does not matter as all we are trying to do is to help them not to be inhibited, and to say what they wish, however little.*)

3   The mayor walking around the village and then stopping either to announce or read out his proclamation about the competition to be held in the village – whoever grows the biggest turnip will win the prize of the spotted cow. (*Once again all the children can make the announcement in their own words; some of them may cup their hands over their mouths.*)

4   The rain and sun – moving as the rain which falls on the turnip seed the farmer has planted; moving as the sun spreading its warmth over the seed to help it grow.

5   The village neighbours – divide into groups of five; in each group there is a farmer, wife, policeman, dustman and milkman. (*All groups work at the same time.*) The farmer pulls but cannot move the turnip, calls his wife, they both try, she calls the milkman and all three try; he calls the dustman who suggests trying to dig around it; they all try but it is no use. He calls the policeman who suggests tying a rope around the turnip and they all pull and finally fall over. (*The numbers in the group may be varied and other characters added or substituted*, e.g. a soldier; a cat; a dog; a postman; a mouse; a grandson/daughter.)

6   The spotted cow – all move as the spotted cow, then divide into groups of six. Each group walks in procession having chosen how they will carry their turnip, e.g. push it in a big wheelbarrow, carry it in a large sheet, pull it along the ground. Each group wins a cow and all dance to celebrate.

Using percussion instruments

Assemble a drum, tambourine, shakers, woodblock, maraca, bells, etc. Divide into six groups. In turns the groups will use the instruments while the others move. Not every part of the story needs music but the following could be tried:

1   Galloping rhythm for the farmer and wife going to the village
2   A slow marching rhythm for the mayor
3   Quick light rhythm for the rain
4   A slow continuous sound for the sun
5   A gay happy rhythm for the end.

At the beginning the teacher can start a rhythm and gradually bring in the children until she feels she can stop playing; percussion work to accompany drama work is very free and no tunes are asked for, so the teacher who is not music-trained need not feel she cannot do this work with her children. However, if the teacher is musical and has taught her class some simple melodies she can take advantage of this in her drama class. Here is a simple tune for piano which the children could accompany on their percussion while the farmer and his wife gallop to market. Words could be added to the tune.

Gallop in C

Arranging the hall

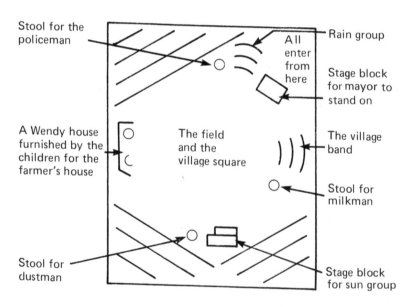

A possible sequence
(*Divide up class and have farmer in his field, wife in the house, milkman, dustman and policeman sitting on their stools, groups for sun sitting on their stage blocks and the town band and the mayor and spotted cow ready to enter in procession. A few of the children who will play instruments could be sitting from the beginning in the band corner.*)

Once upon a time there was a poor farmer who worked hard in his little field all day. While he was digging with his spade his wife was busy in their little house. (*We watch the various occupations done by the farmer and his wife.*) At last it was time for the poor farmer to go home for his supper. (*The farmer returns home, his wife gives him his supper, they eat and talk. Finally they decide to go to the village. The music group play and sing to accompany them as they move round in a big circle arriving at the village square.*) When the poor farmer and his wife arrived at the village they saw the town band and the mayor coming. (*Other characters could join the farmer and his wife, and they all watch the town band playing and marching in procession followed by the mayor. The band sits with the other music group and the mayor climbs up on his block to announce the competition.*) 'We are going to have a competition. You have to grow a turnip. If you grow the biggest turnip you will win a prize – this lively spotted cow.' (*The mayor sits down with the cow and all the people go home.*) The poor farmer and his wife went back to their little field. They planted the turnip seeds very carefully . . . and then went home. . . . All through the summer the turnip seeds grew. On some days it rained. (*Music group begins to play rain accompaniment and the rain group moves about freely before returning to its own place.*) And on other days the sun would shine, spreading its warmth and helping the seeds to grow. Just look at the sun coming up! (*Sun group slowly rises and moves all over, making big magical circles over the seeds as the music group plays slowly.*) But in the evening the sun would slowly go away . . . (*returning to place*) and sink down into the sky. At long last the day of the competition came and the poor farmer went to his field to look at his turnips. (*Farmer looks up and down the rows or walks around, pulls out a few. They are too small and he throws them away. Suddenly he pulls at one which he can't get out.*) The poor farmer threw away the little turnips. They would never win a prize. Then suddenly he got hold of one and he pulled and pulled but he couldn't get it out. So he ran to call his wife. (*The farmer calls his wife, they try to pull the turnip out. In the following sequence a neighbour, e.g. the milkman, is told what has happened. He makes suggestions and then calls another neighbour and so on.*) They all stood in a long line ready to pull. Will you all help them by saying 'pull'! (*All the children watching join in and the noise grows to a climax.*) Are you ready? Pull! . . . Pull! . . . Pull! Once again 'Pull!' and they all fell down! (*The music group will probably want to make one big bang as the farmer and his neighbours fall down.*) There was the biggest, fattest turnip the poor farmer had ever seen. (*If the children are really involved in the story the contrast in*

*atmosphere from the excitement to a still hush will happen quite natur-
ally.*) Everyone crowded round to have a look at it. They had never
seen such an enormous turnip before. (*They chat among themselves
deciding how to carry it. The whole group moves round the room
travelling to the village. As they move a trolley covered in turnips of
all shapes and sizes could be slipped in beside the mayor sitting on his
stage block.*) At last they arrived at the village. The mayor looked at
all the other turnips . . . and then at the poor farmer's turnip. (*Mayor
stands on his stage block.*) He is going to say who has won the competition. (*Mayor says,* 'The farmer has won! This is the biggest
turnip. Here is the spotted cow for you.') Was the mayor right? Is
the farmer's turnip the biggest and best one? (*Children watching
shout* 'Yes'.) The village band is going to play so that the farmer, his
wife and all his friends can dance. Will you join in and clap your
hands while they dance for you? (*The music group plays a gay rhythm,
e.g. a skipping rhythm, as all the children dance including the sun and
rain groups. Finally they all go off leaving just the sound of music.*)

Other examples
The Secret Shoemakers by James Reeves – a selection of Grimm's
Tales (Puffin)
Jack and the Beanstalk; Sleeping Beauty; Twelve Dancing Princesses –
Ladybird Books
First Folk Tales by Mollie Clarke – a selection from different countries
(Rupert Hart-Davis).

A selection of books containing traditional folk, fairy and modern stories
Tell Me Another Story; Time for a Story; My First Big Story Book –
Young Puffin
7-Minute Tales by Rhoda Power; *10-Minute Tales* by Rhoda Power;
Let's Have a Story by M. Bingley – Evans
*Stories for Five Year Olds; Stories for Six Year Olds; Stories for
Seven Year Olds* by S. S. Corrin – Faber

A selection of individual stories suitable for dramatization
Doctor Sean by P. Breinburg and Errol Lloyd: Bodley Head

Farmer Barnes and the Snow Picnic by J. Cunliffe and J. Hickson:
André Deutsch
Benjy's Dog House by M. B. Graham: Bodley Head
The Wind Blew by P. Hutchins: Bodley Head
The Railway Passage by C. Keeping: Oxford University Press
The Witch in the Cherry Tree by M. Mahy and J. Williams: Dent

Wolf! Wolf! by E. and G. Rose: Faber
Skimpy by W. Sansom and H. Abrahams: André Deutsch
Nate the Great by M. W. Sharmat: World's Work

Other sources
1 Ballet stories – *Coppelia; Nutcracker; La Boutique Fantasque.*
2 Musical stories – *Sorcerer's Apprentice; Peter and the Wolf.*
3 Stories by famous writers – *Tale of Peter Rabbit, Tailor of Gloucester* etc. by Beatrix Potter; *The Ugly Duckling* etc. by Hans Andersen; *Alice in Wonderland* by Lewis Carroll; *Winnie the Pooh, The House at Pooh Corner* by A. A. Milne.
   An example is given below.

The Selfish Giant by Oscar Wilde
(Freely adapted from *The Happy Prince and Other Stories* by Oscar Wilde.)
(The children can be told the story either in their classroom or while they interpret it in movement and mime, as in Chapter 1. An adapted plot is given here in brief.)
   Once there was a beautiful garden where trees of all kinds grew. During the summer time the hot sun would shine on the trees warming all the leaves on the branches. But there was a high stone wall all around the garden and a big sign saying KEEP OUT. One day the children who lived in the village came and crept round the wall – they were searching for a way into the garden. Suddenly one of the children found a small hole in the wall and they all crawled through. When they were in the beautiful garden they played games and enjoyed themselves. What they didn't know was that a giant (*An old man could be an alternative.*) owned the garden. A giant who hated children. So all the time the children were playing the giant was in his house, and when he looked out of the window what did he see? (*Children will reply.*) What did he do? (*Various suggestions will be offered.*) He gave a great roar and rushed out of his house shouting at the children to get out. They all ran back through the hole in the wall and the giant went back to his house. Soon it was winter and the snow fell covering the whole garden. The cold wind blew leaving icicles hanging, and the giant was cold and restless. At long last spring came to the village but in the giant's garden it was still winter. 'Why is winter so long this year?' wondered the giant, 'I wish spring would come.' But all was cold and white in the giant's garden. Then while the giant slept he dreamed he heard some beautiful music. (*Play music either on a record player or from a tape, and let it run for a short*

while. A possible piece of music is *The Swan of Tuonela* by Sibelius or 'Morning' from *Peer Gynt Suite* by Grieg; just a few bars are all that are needed.) The sound of the beautiful music melted the giant's cold, selfish heart and when he awoke he felt sorry for being so unkind to the children. 'I wish they would come back,' he said. 'I'm so lonely all on my own.' And as he spoke he looked out of the window and the snow melted and the sun shone on the trees bringing spring into the giant's garden. The giant was so happy he ran to the high wall and called the children. 'Come into my garden – help me knock down the wall – I am sorry I was so unkind.' All the children helped the giant and the high wall fell down and the giant welcomed the children into his garden.

Working in groups
A simple division would be to have one group as the giant and one for the children.
A more elaborate division would be to have six groups:
1   The trees in the garden
2   The sun
3   The giant
4   The children
5   The snow
6   The cold wind

Percussion instruments
A drum, woodblock and tambourine would be sufficient to accompany the story.

The setting and the sequence

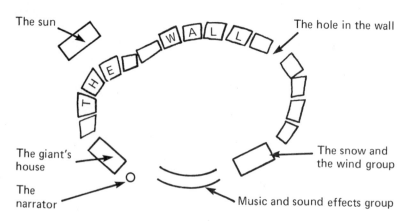

A very simple setting can quickly be arranged as in the diagram by collecting a number of cardboard boxes and cartons. These should either be painted or have the kind of wallpaper stuck on them that gives the effect of brick or stone. (*Wallpaper of this kind is easily obtained.*) This is all that is really necessary except for a stage block placed outside the wall for the sun group to stand on (*One class wanted the sun to be high up*); and two lower levels used for the giant's house and the snow and wind groups to sit on and watch from *{At a later stage when the class wanted just one giant and his wife another level was brought in and the teacher as narrator sat on it. A group around her played instruments and made sound effects for the appropriate parts of the story. The tree group who had originally been scattered within the circle were now either playing instruments or being children as the class had decided that they would imagine the trees in the garden.*)

The order of events given below is just one possible sequence:

1 Trees grow up in the garden.
2 Sun comes up, spreads warmth as the trees bend and sway.
3 Children creep around searching for a hole in the wall. All enter the garden. Some play games, others picnic etc.
4 Giant rushes out shouting, chases them away and returns to house.
5 Winter comes – snow falls, cold wind blows – trees become cold and stiff.
6 Giant sleeps and hears music. Wakes. Runs to call children.
7 Children and giant knock down the wall. Children welcomed into the garden.

Comment

After the initial telling of the story using the basic plot as given above, the children improvised the story using movement, mime and speech. Teachers noted that the children then freely offered their own variations on the basic plot: one class wished the giant to have a wife, another that one of the children should be trapped in the garden. These ideas were accepted and incorporated into the dramatization at the second telling, so that the story really became the children's and this is a development that should always be encouraged. One class enjoyed the story so much that it produced endless variations, and new developments occurred at each telling.

A different sequence from the one given above was tried out. The children were asked to bring a cardboard box to school, and in one classroom session the wall was built by each child working on his/her own box to turn it into part of a brick wall. Then in the following lesson the boxes were all taken into the hall and arranged together to form the wall. The class was divided into two groups: those outside the wall, the children; those inside, the giant. The story was told and the children responded in movement and speech. They found it easy to be the giant shouting angrily (each child here was encouraged to think what he was going to call out – in this way a wider variety of ideas was encouraged) but they found it more difficult to think of a variety of things to say as the giant speaking kindly at the end, and a discussion about this was needed.

Setting the story with an audience

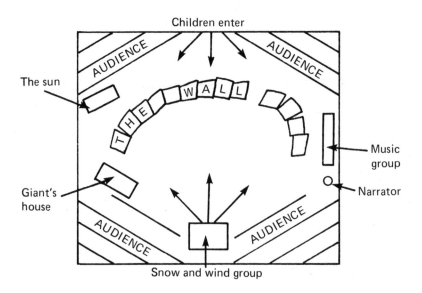

Presenting to an audience

Occasions occur when teachers are asked to present something dramatic to an audience, usually the parents of the children. Sometimes the best work shown is that which has arisen out of work done during the term, rather than something specially prepared in a very short time.

Ideally the audience should sit either in the round or in a semi-circle, with the children performing close to them, and not on stage from where it is often extremely difficult to hear. In fact the setting should be as near as possible the same as when they were working without an audience, so that those watching are placed in positions which fit in with what the children need and are used to.

Costumes, props and settings should be kept to the minimum and be simple, colourful and lightweight, so as not to hamper them. Blocks and steps can be used to build up levels, and entrances and exits are through gaps in the audience. When they are not actually performing, children can sit within the circle so that they still feel part of the whole production.

To avoid tension and fear about not remembering lines, scripts should never be given to them; if a child is not well on the day it is then possible for another to take his place quite easily.

Many of the stories already mentioned in this chapter are suitable both for work during the term and for presentation. A few examples are given here which I have found particularly appropriate to the Christmas term:

The story of the Nutcracker ballet
The Sleeping Beauty
The Tailor of Gloucester, by Beatrix Potter
The Silver Horse, by Ursula Moray Williams (in *Time for a Story* – Young Puffin)
The Unkind Prince – a traditional tale (in *Stories to Play in the Infant School* by Lilian McCrea)
The Fir Tree, by Hans Andersen
Dick Whittington.

Examples more suitable for the summer term and for out-of-doors are:

The story of Noah and the Ark
Pinocchio
Snow-White
*Jack and the Beanstalk ⎫
The Mummers' Play ⎬ obtainable on one record
*The Pied Piper ⎫
Alice in Wonderland ⎬ obtainable on one record

*Versions of these stories have been recorded by the author on two BBC records RESR13 and RESR33S. The recordings contain free adaptations of the stories with narration, music and details of presentation. They can be used for listening to as an end in itself, or they can be a starting point for the children's own version of the stories.

5   *Speech*

A child's intellectual ability is not the only controlling factor in his acquisition of spoken language. Speech is one of the most spontaneous outlets of his emotional life. His facility in speech develops most smoothly when he is secure and happy, and encouraged, by the sympathetic understanding and reception of his efforts, to use speech freely.

(Report of the Advisory Council of Education in Scotland)

In this chapter we will be looking at different ways in which we can help children to develop oral fluency and so communicate their thoughts and ideas. Often work in speech is rather haphazard, so it is not surprising that many teachers find that while children are happy doing mime and movement, they are much less confident when it comes to using speech. Some children have difficulty in speaking either in the drama class or in the classroom. So alongside the verbal work which is inherent in improvisation, storymaking and dramatization, the child needs other lessons where the emphasis is solely on speech.

Considerations when planning a lesson

The young child learns to speak through listening, copying, making his own attempts to talk and through correction. However, many children are deprived of any real chance of listening and talking because of a lack of opportunity for conversation at home. It is not just that once they have started school they often have difficulty in coping with the mechanics of speech, but rather that their imagination, ideas and thoughts may have been starved or stifled. Oral fluency can only develop if a child is given plenty of opportunities to express himself. In copying what he hears at home or in school he will copy good speech and bad speech. The teacher of drama, being aware of this, should ensure that her own diction is clear and pleasant in tone. Lazy, slovenly diction, and harsh or ugly tones, are only too easy to copy. There is of course no suggestion that teachers should attempt to eradicate genuine local or regional dialects, or that there is only one correct way of speaking or one accent which is socially acceptable. What matters is that the speaker should be heard clearly and understood, and that her tone of voice should be pleasant to listen to.

Ideas for lessons

Some of the ideas are suitable for very short periods; others can be developed into project work over a number of weeks. Some are for solo work, others are more suitable for small groups and whole class involvement.

1 *Class television programme* (suitable for class project)
The lead-up to this is done in a series of items:
(a) Telling the news
   The children tell their news, which is usually of personal interest; then the teacher widens this by relating some school news or tells of something she has seen happening on her way to school. For children who are less confident I suggest they bring a picture or object to show the others and talk to them about. (When this class television programme idea was tried out with a group of children, one girl brought a series of pictures she had drawn, and her friend held them up as she told a story she had made up.)
(b) 'Hobbies corner'
   This could begin with the teacher showing, say, a new set of stamps or a model car or a doll, and encouraging those children who like stamps or have lots of cars or dolls to talk about theirs.
(c) Animals
   Again this could begin with the teacher talking to the children about animals and then letting them take over the talking as various topics are discussed, e.g. if someone was given a cat or a dog as a new pet, how should they look after it? 'What do animals do in the winter time?'
(d) Miscellaneous items
   (All tried out as above.) The weather today; holidays; puzzles; making things; birthdays.
   After a good deal of oral work suggest to the children that they have their own television programme. The Wendy House (with the roof

removed) can be used as the studio, its window serving as the screen. The teacher, speaking from inside the house, introduces the programme and links the items together. Later the children do this: 'Good morning everyone, this is Class 2's Tuesday programme – here is the news.' (Individual children tell their news and then sit near the Wendy House, leaving it free for the next child.) The teacher introduces the next item and so on, using as many of the children as she can in the lesson (she draws upon the things talked about in the lead-up lessons); the others will have a turn next time. It is important to encourage the children to talk using any type of visual aid they want; this helps the less confident, and makes it more interesting to those watching and listening. It does not matter how short the items are. Each child is communicating at his own level, and those who are watching should be allowed to question the speakers if they want to. This may happen as the children become involved, and the question and answer time should prove most valuable. Children do not think it odd that they can talk to those who are, as it were, on screen.

If a class really enjoys this idea it can become a regular feature in the weekly timetable. The number of topics for talking is unlimited.

2 'Remember-remember' (suitable for small groups)
This is the well-known game of putting objects on a tray, looking at them, covering them and then trying to remember what they were.

3 'Feel and say' (suitable for small groups)
Objects of different shapes, weights, textures and smells are put into a bag (e.g. fir cone, cake of soap, paper-weight, bag of crisps). Each child picks out one and has to try to describe it.

4 'Word-game' (suitable for the whole class)
One after the other the children quickly name the things they see about them (anyone who hesitates is out). Then a descriptive word is added (and anyone who uses a word already used is out). Finally a full sentence must be spoken. This game should stimulate quick thinking and, as they laugh and drop out, it all goes very quickly and can then be repeated. Any child who has dropped out in the early stage then has another try.

5 'Telephoning' (suitable for pairs and small groups)
It is useful to have a couple of toy telephones or discarded real ones obtainable from the GPO. All the children should learn how to answer

their own number and how to dial. This should happen as the teacher rings them up individually, and they take it in turns to handle the telephone and answer.

In pairs all sorts of calls can be made, e.g. asking a friend to come to a party; telephoning a shop. In threes or fours a whole series of calls can be made, e.g. a lady phones her friend to say that there is a cat on her roof – the friend phones the fire-brigade – the fireman phones the vet. Once the children have got the idea of the game they will enjoy thinking of ideas and their suggestions should be used as much as possible.

6   *What am I?* (suitable for individual work)

The teacher gives the children a short description of an animal, a person or object, and they have to guess what it is. At the beginning it is sometimes useful to take the object, perhaps a toy, and let the children discover how, through the use of their senses – by feeling it, looking at it, pressing it or shaking it to find out if it makes a sound – they can build up a much better oral picture of the toy.

7   *Where am I?* (suitable for the whole class)

The teacher describes the place, where she is and asks the children 'Where am I?'. The choice of words and phrases used is important as it helps the children to think imaginatively and to use as wide a vocabulary as possible when giving their description.

8   *Chain stores* (suitable for groups)

The teacher gives each group an exciting start and the children in turn make up their part. They have to use their imaginations quickly, and although some of them will only be able to add a very short piece of their own, others will go on for much longer, elaborating and extending the plot or taking the story off in a quite different direction. At the end one child from each group tries to relate his own group story to the others.

9   *How do you do it?* (suitable for the whole class)

The aim here is to enable the children to think clearly so that they can explain simply how something is done using visual aids of any kind.

10   *What did I see?* (suitable for solo work)

In this exercise the children, having observed closely either a person or a happening, must then report it to the class. In this way observation, memory and speech are all stimulated.

11   *Messages* (suitable for pairs or small groups)
This popular game of giving a message, which is then passed on and retold, is a useful one for listening, remembering and accurate retelling.

12   *What can you hear?* (suitable for the whole class)
In turn, the children listen and say what they hear. Begin by asking them to be very quiet so that they can listen to the natural sounds around them, whether in the classroom, in the corridor or outside. The teacher can make sounds herself or play a sound-effect record for the children to identify the sounds. A series of sounds can be used to make up an oral story. A short piece of music can also be played, and the class asked to say what they think is happening in the music. Later they can be asked to close their eyes and imagine they are in the garden at home, or on the beach, at the railway station etc., and then to say what they can hear happening.

13   *Puppets* (suitable for small groups)
Puppets have been made and used in infant schools for many years. They prove again and again that the less verbally skilled child is able to join in and extend his creative powers. Very often a play based on a theme or story he has already experienced in movement is the most fruitful, and helps to release the spoken word. Children also learn quickly that they cannot all speak together when performing a puppet play, and this experience in sharing is useful for social training.

14   *Exhibitions* (suitable for class project)
The children are asked to bring something old from home and to tell the others about it. When a number of interesting objects have been collected a small exhibition of 'odds and ends' is arranged and the children whose objects have been chosen become the museum keepers, while the others come to view and question. This will often lead to an exhibition involving a whole class, e.g. wooden toys, mechanical objects. Each child has a role either as a museum keeper, or a ticket seller, or a guard etc., and another form is invited to visit the exhibition.

15   *'A day in the life of . . .'* (suitable for class project)
As with the previous idea, this involves inviting children from other

classes. The most successful example of this I have seen was entitled 'A day in the life of our class'. The class kept a diary of the day's events; individual children were given their own tasks; the teacher took photographs illustrating the events the children wanted to have recorded, and the natural sounds of the day were put on tape. Then the photographs were presented as in a film show, and certain children were chosen to give the running commentary. The result was a programme using visual material, speech and sounds.

16   'Our newspaper' (suitable for groups)

This idea is a good one if the teacher wants to link her speech and written work. It is in essence complementary to the classroom television programme idea. The children are shown some newspapers, and sheets of paper are prepared with a heading, date etc. With the younger children most of the newspaper will consist of drawings and only a little writing, but with the older ones a paper can be produced each week by a team of editor and reporters who meet to discuss what they will have in their edition. The reporters 'interview' the other children to get news and ideas, and then when all the material is collected the week's team write it all out and illustrate it. The pages of the newspaper are marked off in columns, and the topics will vary from week to week. Topics that seem to be used frequently are:

School news
Puzzles
Animal news
Birthdays
Quizzes
Drawings
General news
Stories

Duplicated copies are made and the other classes in the school are asked if they would like to receive a copy each week.

17   Villages and towns (suitable for class project)

An imaginary village or town is created by the class. A pictorial map is drawn when the children have decided what they want in their village or town. Each child chooses the character he would like to be and puts in his or her own house. Streets are named, houses numbered, buildings added. The village or town is now used for speech work, particularly for discussion (e.g. What shall we build in the open space near the church?) and decision making. This idea at a very simple level draws the children's attention to the environment in which they live, although in an imaginary way. Village events can be used in the improvisation classes; stories about the people, descriptions of the characters and what they do can be used for written work.

Speech technique

In the first part of this chapter ideas were given for increasing verbal communication through widening the scope and fluency of language. Although this is of prime importance when considering speech with young classes, many teachers become aware that some of their children use distorted speech sounds and so become very difficult to understand. When articulation is hampered in this way they need to hear the correct sound and to repeat it until they can use it spontaneously. The degree of distortion varies and if the teacher is uncertain she should ensure that the child concerned visits a speech therapist. However, many young children do not need the help of a speech therapist but simply lots of practice in articulation, which strengthens the organs used in making speech sounds (e.g. lips and tongue), and help in correcting the distortions. The longer this is delayed the more difficult it becomes, as the child gets older, to cope with the psychological problems involved in becoming aware that he needs special help. With the young child who finds great joy and satisfaction in making sounds it is so much easier and more enjoyable to work on the mechanics of speech. This work is of considerable value for all children, not just those who have difficulties.

Practising speech rhymes

These should be presented so as to avoid endless repetition by the children sitting at their desks. A variety of methods can be used which incorporate the use of speech rhymes and give the children a feel of the rhythm in them. (Further work on rhythm is considered in Chapter 6.)

1 Beating or clapping the rhythm while saying the rhyme.
2 Actions to accompany the words. (For the imaginative use of word and action or verbal dynamics see Chapter 6.)
3 Linking various sounds together under a theme, e.g. at a picnic, the zoo, a journey by train to a harbour; a simple story can be told incorporating such sounds as the buzzing of bees, the cooing of doves (croo, croo), braying of donkeys (ee-aw, ee-aw), sound of trains (ch, ch, ch ch) and the 'put . . . put . . . put' of motorboats.

4 Moving as an animal, e.g. a cow, and making noises; then varying the quality of the noise according to how the cow feels – angry, hungry, sad, happy. Other emotive words can be used to give the children practice in extending their vocal range.

5 Conveying a sense of distance and nearness through the use of speech rhymes, for example one about drummer boys, or moving feet. This gives the children practice in the projection of sounds. A simple cueing device is to hold a pencil level when the sound is far away, moving it up as the sound comes nearer and dropping it down again when it goes away.

6 Moving as mechanical things and making the sounds (for example, a clock, a top) and then saying the rhyme, helps with variety of pace.

Length of lesson
It is more beneficial to the children to have a short practice, perhaps five minutes each day, than half an hour once a week.

Speech rhymes
Sounds made with the tip of tongue are T, D, N, L, R, S.

T – *Clocks and Watches*
Our great
Steeple clock
Goes TICK-TOCK,
TICK-TOCK;

Our small
Mantel clock
Goes TICK-TACK- TICK-TACK,
TICK-TACK, TICK-TACK;

Our little
Pocket watch
Goes Tick-a-tacker, tick-a-tacker,
Ticker-a-tacker, tick.

D – *Dilly-dally*
Dilly-dally, dilly-dally,
What a slow-coach is your Sally!
Dawdling through the fields at playtime,
Dreaming drowsy dreams in day-time,
Dilly-dally, dilly-dally,
What a slow-coach is your Sally.

N – *Insey Winsey Spider*
Insey Winsey Spider
Climbs up the spout
Down came the rain and
Washed the Spider out.
Out came the sun,
Dried up all the rain,
Insey Winsey Spider,
Climbs up again.

L – *The Two Rabbits*
Lippy and Loppy are two little rabbits.
   Lippety loppety lippety lop.
All down the long field they go through the stubble,
   Then lippety loppety back to the top.
   Lippety loppety, down to the bottom,
   Lippety loppety, back to the top.
   Lippety loppety, loppety lippety,
     Lippety loppety,
     Lippety
     Lop.

R – *Windy Nights*
Rumbling in the chimneys,
   Rattling at the doors,
Round the roofs and round the roads
   The rude wind roars,
Raging through the darkness,
   Raving through the trees,
Racing off again across
   The great grey seas.

S – *Handy Spandy*
Handy Spandy, Jack-a-dandy,
Loved plum cake and sugar-candy,
He bought some at the grocer's shop,
And out he came, hop, hop, hop.

Sounds made by the back of the tongue are K, G, Ng.

K – *Kan-Kan-Kangaroo*
Kan-Kan-Kangaroo
Hops across the vale;
Flip go his hind legs
And flop goes his tail.

Bouncing through the bushland
Hip-hop-hop,
Kan-Kan-Kangaroo
Can't can't stop!

G – *Gaffer Gilpin*
Gaffer Gilpin got a goose and gander.
Did Gaffer Gilpin get a goose and gander?
If Gaffer Gilpin got a goose and gander,
Where are the goose and gander
　　　that Gaffer Gilpin got?

Ng – *Sing Sing*
Sing, sing, what shall I sing?
The cat has taken the pudding-bag string.
Do, do, what shall I do?
The cat has bitten it right in two.

Sounds made by the lips are P, B, M, Wh.

P – *Higgledy Piggledy*
Higgledy piggledy
　　　Here we lie,
Picked and plucked
　　　And put in a pie!

B – *Washing Day*
　　　I rub and I rub
　　　At the tub, tub, tub,
The clothes in the suds to scrub, scrub, scrub.
　　　But when they are clean,
　　　And white to be seen,
I'll dress like a lady, and dance on the green.

M – *Misty Moisty Morning*
One misty moisty morning,
When cloudy was the weather,
There I met an old man,
Dressed all in leather;
I took him by the hand,
And told him very plain,
How do you, how do you do?
And how do you do again?

Wh – *What's the weather?*
Whether the weather be fine,
Or whether the weather be not,
Whether the weather be cold,
Or whether the weather be hot –
We'll weather the weather,
Whatever the weather,
Whether we like it or not.

Sounds made with the teeth and tongue are Sh, Ch, J, F, V, Th.

Sh – *Hippity, hippity hop*
A hippity, hippity hop! Heigh-ho!
Away to the blacksmith's shop we go.
If you have a pony
That's lost a shoe,
You can get her another
All shining and new.
A hippity, hippity hop!

Ch – *The Woodman*
    Chip chop, chip chop,
The Woodman with his chopper chops,
    Chip chop, chip chop,
Stout and strong and proper chops.

On beeches, oaks and larches, too,
    His hatchet brightly rings,
And while he chops so cheerily,
    As cheerily he sings.

'Chip chop, chip chop,
Stout and strong and proper chops.
      Chip chop, chip chop.
The Woodman with his chopper chops'.

J – *Just like me*
I went up one pair of stairs
      Just like me.
I went up two pairs of stairs
      Just like me.
I went into a room
      Just like me.
I looked out of a window
      Just like me.

F – *Feet*
      Big feet
      Black feet
Going up and down the street;
      Dull and shiny
      Father's feet,
      Walk by me.

      Nice feet
      Brown feet
Going up and down the street;
      Pretty, dainty,
      Ladies' feet
      Trip by me!

      Small feet,
      Light feet,
Going up and down the street
      Little children's
      Happy feet
      Run by me!

V – *Uncle Vic*
My Uncle Vic
He has a van
He is a very lucky man.

When I am rich
Ten years from now,
I'll have a van like his, I vow!

Th – *Feathers*
Birds have feathers.
Father said, 'Who else has feathers?'
'Cats?' No feathers.
'Dogs?' No feathers.
'Lions and tigers?' No – no feathers.
'Elephants?' No – no feathers.
'Cows then?' No, they don't have feathers.
Father thought of everything
But only birds have feathers.

Sounds which often cause problems are L, R and S when combined
with other sounds.

Bl – *A Blanket*
If a blanket you should blot,
With a blemish, mark or spot,
Bleach the blanket, bleach it white,
And put it on the bed at night.

Cl – *What a clatter*
In the classroom,
What a clatter,
I wonder what
Can be the matter.

Clashing, banging,
Clinking, clanking.
I think those children
Need a spanking.

Sl – *Slippers*
In my slippers I can slide,
Right down Mummy's hall I glide.
Mummy says, 'Don't slide that way,
Or you will slip and fall one day.'

Fl – *This little fly*
This little fly in a terrible flurry.
Flustering right round the room in a hurry.
I feel he must realize without any doubt,
That we're opening the window to fling him out.

Gl – *My Glove*
I have lost my right hand glove,
But I am not sad,
For I had lost my left hand glove,
And so I am quite glad.

Dr – *Drummer Boys*
Drummer boys are drumming
D-d-d-d-rum, d-d-d-d-rum, d-d-d-d-rum, d-d-d-d-rum.
Drummer boys are marching,
Drumming, here they come;
Marching, drumming, brightly drumming,
D-d-d-d-rum, d-d-d-d-rum, d-d-d-d-rum, d-d-d-d-rum
Let us join the drummer boys
And d-d-d-d-rum, d-d-d-d-rum, d-d-d-d-rum.

Br – *Bridges*
That old bridge was made of brick,
Many years ago.
Then it crossed a little brook,
That wandered clear and slow.

That new bridge is made of steel,
A river broad to span,
It shines so brightly in the sun,
A marvel made by man.

Tr – *Donkey*
Trot little donkey, trot, trot, trot,
Your supper is waiting, so trot, trot, trot,
Carrots for you and oats, a fine lot,
So trot little donkey, trot, trot, trot.

Gr – *The Grumpy Grandfather*
Grandfather Dumps
Grizzles and grumps
And grouses and grumbles
As if he had mumps;
Grouses and grumbles
And grizzles and grumps.
I'm glad we are strangers
Glum Grandfather Dumps.

Cr – *Criss-Cross*
Criss, cross, cross, criss
The cutting scissors look like this.

Creak, crick, crick, creak,
The little duck is going to speak.

Crick, crack, crack, crick,
The shell is breaking, out comes chick.

St – *The Butcher's Shop*
There are strings and strings of sausages in the butcher's shops,
Besides the strings of sausages, beef-steaks and mutton chops.

Sp – *Splish Splosh*
Splish splosh, splish splosh!
Through the puddles Tom is sploshing.
Splish splosh, splish splosh!
Won't young Tommy need a washing.

Sw – *Sweeping*
Sweep, sweep, sweep,
Sweep with a swish of the broom;
Sweep at the centre, sweep at the side,
Sweep every inch of the room.

Sweep, sweep, sweep,
Sweep from the window to the door;
Sweep by the chest, sweep by the chair,
Sweep as you've never swept before!

Sn – *Snow*
Snow, snow, glorious snow!
On our toboggan down we go.
Swooping and flying over the snow.
Isn't it glorious out in the snow.

Sl – *Sleepy head*
'Come, let's to bed', says Sleepy-head;
'Tarry a while', says Slow.
'Put on the pan', says greedy Nan,
'Let's sup before we go.'

6 Poetry

There is no recipe for producing readers who will enjoy poetry, but there are plenty of ingredients that will take young people from their first gleeful enjoyment of jingles and assonance and funny noise up to the time when adult poetry becomes accessible. School and home together can create an ambience in which poetry is normal and necessary. And if young readers can be young writers as well, so much the better; nothing brings to life the worth and craftsmanship of adult poetry so vividly as a young poet's own effort to say what he wants to.

D. Thompson   *Poetry for Children*

Although the writer in the above passage is thinking more of older children than of those in the infant school, it is in the infant school that most of them will first be introduced to poetry. In this chapter three ways by which this introduction can be achieved will be considered. First, through the speaking of poetry; second, by the children creating their own poems; and third, by the teacher herself reading poems to them.

Speaking poetry

Many people do not like group speaking but with young children it can be great fun. It is easy for them to learn the words because they do so by listening and repeating, not by having to read them. It is probably better not to have the whole group speaking the entire poem in unison, which is difficult, but only certain lines. This helps to avoid monotonous chanting. Initially a child has only to remember his own bit, and the shyer ones gain in confidence by being in a group.

A study of the construction of a poem will show how it can be divided up for group work and solo voices. For example, some poems are written on a question and answer pattern or have a refrain line, and here the division could be a simple two- or three-part one. Often the images are built on a regular pattern throughout the poem, in which case there will be as many small groups as there are images; a poem may build to a climax so that, as more and more voices join in, a cumulative effect is produced. When the images appear to be irregular then the divisions are done accordingly.

Besides dividing the poem up for speaking the class itself should be physically grouped in such a way that the full sound of the poem is heard. Children enjoy, for example, standing and sitting on or in a boat or a train they have made if the poem concerns it, or being grouped on levels based on plans like those below (rather than sitting at their desks).

Poems done chorally often seem to need some form of movement, and the young ones naturally like to do this. How much action there is will depend on the poem itself, but generally speaking it is better to keep it to a minimum so that it does not distract from the spoken word.

Before beginning a poem many teachers find that it helps to do a little preliminary work, otherwise the poem has to be repeated again and again and the children get tired of it. It is better to do this with rhythm rhymes and through the use of a simple form of verbal dynamics.

Rhythm rhymes

It is useful to have a few percussion instruments to hand. The rhythm rhymes can be done in a variety of ways. Sometimes the teacher can play the beat in the rhyme on one of the percussion instruments, then the children move to the beat; she may speak the rhyme while the children move; a small group then try out the rhythm on the percussion instruments; one group can speak the rhyme while another moves and a third plays the instruments. The rhymes can be broken up rather than spoken in unison, and if one group is moving vigorously then it is probably better that another group is speaking. Once the children have tried a few, a rhyme can be done as a 'round', so that they have to listen really hard. A teacher's constant aim is to help them to enjoy the sense of rhythm, the quality of lightness, or strength, the change of pace and volume, and onomatopoeic words.

For those teachers who would like to extend their children's experience in rhythm and sound a very useful book is *Musical Activities with Young Children* by Jean Gilbert (Ward Lock Educational). The book is full of practical ideas on how to use percussion instruments and gives details on how to make them.

A selection of rhymes
Walking
Follow-my-leader, follow-my-leader,
Follow-my-leader after me.
Follow me up to the top of the hill
And follow me down to the sea.

Skipping
If you can skip on the tip of your toes
I'll give you a ribbon to tie into bows,
Skip, skip, for everyone knows
It's easy to skip on the tip of your toes.

Marching
Left, right, left, right
Hear the tramping feet;
A regiment has come to town
Marching down the street.

Hopping
Moppety-Moppit
And Poppety-Pop
Went on their way
With a skip and a hop –
One with a skip,
One with a hop
Moppety-Moppit
And Poppety-Pop!

Swinging
Swing me high,
Swing me low,
Swing me up to the sky O.
Swing me high,
Swing me low,
Swing me down to the ground O.

Jumping
I can bounce,
I can roll,
I can hop, skip and jump
I can dodge,
I can leap,
I can fly, bound and bump.

I can prance,
I can dance,
I can run, spin and fall,
I can glide,
I can slide,
I'm a jolly rubber ball.

Galloping
Bell horses, bell horses,
    What time of day?
One o'clock, two o'clock,
    Three and away.

Rowing
Row, boatman, row!
Row, boatman, row!
Over the foam and far from home,
Row, boatman, row!

For pace, volume and onomatopoeic words:
Look out!
Look out, look out, a motor is coming!
Look out, look out, a motor is coming!
Here it comes splashing
And hooting and dashing
Look out, look out, look out!

Rush hour
What a rush,
What a crush,
What a fuss, fuss, fuss!
Everybody's running for the 5 o'clock bus.

What a hustle,
What a tussle,
What a bustle, bustle, bustle!
Till every seat is full
On the five o'clock bus.

Word and movement or verbal dynamics

This idea of speaking a word and performing the movement or action simultaneously has been called verbal dynamics (Burniston and Bell 1972). It is a method of helping children to make their speech come alive and their movement freer. If used before they start the choral work it will stimulate a more imaginative response in them, and the words in the poem are less likely to sound toneless, but should be full of the vigour of their meaning. This word and movement work, together with speech and rhythm rhymes, help children to enjoy speaking verse.

Having chosen a poem one isolates two or three words from it and works on them separately. One may even perform the action and say the words in a situation which is not in the poem at all. The word should be spoken at the same time as the movement is carried out. For example, with the words *scattered* and *roar* which appear in the poem 'Snowflakes' below, the children could try performing the action of scattering corn to feed chickens as they say 'scatter, scatter, scatter'. It will be seen immediately how the sharp repeated sounds of *s*, *k*, *t*, in the word fit the action of scattering perfectly. With the word *roar* the children can try being lions and saying the word 'roar', 'roar' as they move; the *r* and the long *oar* sounds done simultaneously with the action are then given their full value and are not cut short. Having done this for a little while the poem is then spoken (*without any actions*) and it will be noticeable how much more vital the children's speech is.

A selection of poems suitable for choral speaking
Snowflakes
See the snowflakes twirling, twisting,
See them dancing all around.
Watch the snowflakes gently falling
Watch them floating to the ground.

Hear the wind come madly rushing,
Hear it roar along the street.
See the snowflakes blown and scattered,
See them like a great white sheet.

Now the wind is dying slowly,
Now it's peaceful once again.
Now the snowflakes settle gently,
Covering every road and lane.

J. Lambert

The Huntsmen
Three jolly gentlemen,
    In coats of red,
Rode their horses
    Up to bed.

Three jolly gentlemen
    Snored till morn,
Their horses champing
    The golden corn.

Three jolly gentlemen,
    At break of day,
Came clitter-clatter down the stairs
    And galloped away.

Walter de la Mare

Here comes the Band
Listen to the band,
With its rum, tum, tum,
Tiddle tum, tiddle tum,
Tum, tum, tum.

We can make a band
With a rum, tum, tum,
Tiddle tum, tiddle tum,
Tum, tum, tum.

Listen to the band,
With its tootle, tootle, toot.
Tootle, tootle, tootle, tootle,
Tootle, tootle, toot.

We can make a band
With a tootle, tootle, toot.
Tootle, tootle, tootle tootle,
Tootle, tootle, toot.

Maisie Cobby

The Goblin

A goblin lives in our house, in our house, in our house,
A goblin lives in our house all the year round.
    He bumps
    And he jumps
    And he thumps
    And he stumps.
    He knocks
    And he rocks
    And he rattles at the locks.
A goblin lives in our house, in our house, in our house,
A goblin lives in our house all the year round.

                          Rose Fyleman

Train Talk

Clickety-clack! clickety-clack!
Here comes the train along the track.
Chug, chug, choo, chug, chug, choo.
Oh what a fuss and what a to do!
Rickety-rack, rickety-rack,
I can't stay here, I must get back.
Chuff, chuff, choo, chuff, chuff, choo.
Do hurry up! I can't wait for you!
With a wheeze and a sneeze
And a whistle and a cough
Slam goes the door and, hurrah!
    I'm off.

Isn't it Cold!

Clap both your hands.
Jump round about.
Isn't it cold, isn't it cold!
Put on your coat
Let us go out.
Isn't it cold, isn't it cold!

Hark, how the winds
Whistle and blow!
Isn't it cold, isn't it cold!
Look at the ice
Look at the snow
Isn't it cold, isn't it cold!

Pile up the snow.
Make a snow man.
Isn't it cold, isn't it cold!
Make him as big
And fat as you can!
Isn't it cold, isn't it cold!

Put this old hat
On his round head
Isn't it cold, isn't it cold!
Now let's run home
To a warm bed.
Isn't it cold, isn't it cold!

   Oh!
  Isn't it cold!
   Mary Daunt

Bonfire Night

Watch the fireworks whizzing round,
Round and round along the ground.
Up they go into the sky
High, high, so very high.

Watch the jumping-jack go round,
Round and round along the ground.
Watch the rocket going up,
Mounting skywards, up and up.

Take a sparkler, watch it spark,
Sparkling brightly in the dark.
Watch the fire so burning bright,
Blazing warmly in the night.
    R. Brighton

The Little Piggies

Where are you going, you little pig?
I'm leaving my mother, I'm growing so big!
  So big, young pig!
  So young, so big!
What, leaving your mother, you foolish young pig!
Where are you going, you little pig?
I've got a new spade, and I'm going to dig.
  To dig, little pig
  A little pig dig.

Well, I never saw a pig with a spade that could dig!
Where are you going, you little pig?
Why I'm going to have a nice ride in a gig.
　　In a gig, little pig!
　　What, a pig in a gig!
Well, I never saw a pig ride in a gig!
Where are you going, little pig?
I'm going to the barber's to buy a wig.
　　A wig, little pig!
　　A pig in a wig!
Why, whoever before saw a pig in a wig?
Where are you going, you little pig?
Why I'm going to the ball to dance a fine jig.
　　A jig, little pig!
　　A pig dance a jig!
Well, I never saw a pig dance a jig!

Thomas Hood

The Cats Have Come to Tea
What did she see – oh, what did she see,
As she stood leaning against the tree?
Why, all the cats had come to tea.

What a fine turnout from roundabout!
All the houses had let them out.
And here they were with scamper and shout.

'Mew, mew, mew!' was all they could say,
And, 'We hope we find you well today.'

Oh, what would she do – oh, what should she do!
What a lot of milk they would get through.
For here they were with, 'Mew, mew, mew!'

She did not know – oh, she did not know,
If bread and butter they'd like or no;
They might want little mice, oh! oh! oh!

Dear me – oh, dear me!
All the cats had come to tea.

Kate Greenaway

Creating poems

One of the most enjoyable ways of doing poetry with young children
is to help them to create their own poems. Generally these poems

will be the work of a whole class rather than an individual child. Poems will not just happen; they need to arise out of some experience the children have had, whether in the drama lesson or outside school. One of the simplest ways of beginning is to give them a short session in movement, doing things related to the subject of the poem. A movement lesson on balloons began with the teacher bringing a bunch of balloons into the hall. The children were free to enjoy themselves with a variety of movements, but were not told what was to happen. Back in the classroom they sat grouped round the teacher and the balloons were looked at, talked about, tossed in the air etc. As the children replied to her questions, phrases were written on the board, and then finally the lines of the poem were put in the order they wanted. In fact, very little adjustment was needed, and the whole lesson, from the time the children entered the hall and saw the balloons to the completion of the poem, took about half an hour. It was the first time this class had ever tried creating a poem. They were delighted with it and wanted to speak it not just among themselves but to the other children in the school.

Balloons
I like balloons
Pop, bang, crash, wallop
Round like a football, a pear or an egg.
Long like a sausage and a funny clown's head.
Sh – sh – sh – sh –
Growing fatter, growing bigger
Flying, gliding, sailing, bouncing
Floating in the sky.

Use of the senses and refrain lines
If children are to create poems they need plenty of opportunities to increase their awareness of the sense of touch, taste, smell, sight and sound. The method of creating the poem with their teacher can be the same as for balloons. Sometimes the use of a refrain line can be tried as it often gives even the simplest of poems a rhythmic feel. The poems that follow are the work of children aged five–seven. The early efforts tend to be more factual as the children simply note what they have seen; gradually the poems become more descriptive and the refrain line is used less obviously, until finally it is not needed at all, and there is a beautiful use of contrasting images, movement and colour.

The Snowman
He wears a hat and scarf,
He has no arms and legs,
He doesn't move or run
He melts in the sun.

He has a round tummy
And a large head
And stone buttons for eyes,
He melts in the sun.

He has a mouth
And he smokes a pipe
Sometimes he has a broom
Or a walking stick
He melts in the sun.

The Clown
The clown tumbles
The people all laugh,
His trousers are baggy
His braces are slack,
The clown tumbles
He's a very funny chap.

The Witch
The witch is here
You can feel her over your head,
Her broomstick whistles past
Her cat sits at the back,
You can hear a cruel croaking voice
And see a sharp pointed nose
And a tall black hat,
The witch is here.

Christmas Time
When it is winter it feels very cold
Bells are ringing, children singing,
Throwing snowballs at each other,
Bells are ringing, children singing,
Christmas time is a happy time

Bells are ringing, children singing,
Father Christmas has a sackful of toys,
Children singing, singing, singing,
Bells are ringing, ringing, ringing.
Jesus is born on Christmas Day
Bells are ringing, children singing.

The Sea
All kinds of shapes and colours –
                    that is the sea.
All shells are beautiful
Some shells are shining as they glitter
                    in the sun,
All kinds of shapes and colours –
                    that is the sea.
Waves crash against the rocks like thunder,
The waves themselves are moving rocks
                    and mountains,
All kinds of shapes and colours –
                    that is the sea.

This is the Sea
The waving seaweed
    and the rounded cockle shells,
The moving water
    swaying in the wind,
The swimming fish
    which dart and glide,
The golden sand
    as soft as silk,
The silver pebbles
    on the beach,
This is the sea.

Reading poems

I have selected a few poems which I think children will enjoy having read to them. It is of great value to them just to listen to a poem, read simply but with full value given to the images, even if they cannot fully understand it. The poems done chorally and the ones they create are naturally within their imaginative experience, but some of those read to them can be used to widen their horizons.

Mick
>Mick my mongrel-O
>Lives in a bungalow
>Painted green with a round doorway.
>With an eye for cats
>And a nose for rats
>He lives on his threshold half the day.
>He buries his bones
>By the rockery stones
>And never, oh never, forgets the place.
>Ragged and thin
>From his tail to his chin
>He looks at you with a sideways face.
>Dusty and brownish,
>Wicked and clownish,
>He'll win no prize at the County Show.
>But throw him a stick,
>And up jumps Mick,
>And right through the flower-beds see him go!
>>James Reeves

The Snare
>I hear a sudden cry of pain!
>>There is a rabbit in a snare;
>Now I hear the cry again,
>>But I cannot tell from where.
>But I cannot tell from where,
>>He is calling out for aid;
>Crying on the frightened air,
>>Making everything afraid.
>Making everything afraid,
>>Wrinkling up his little face;
>As he cries again for aid,
>>And I cannot find the place!
>And I cannot find the place,
>>Where his paw is in the snare;
>Little one! Oh! little one!
>>I am searching everywhere.
>>James Stephens

Stopping by Woods on a Snowy Evening
Whose woods these are I think I know.
His house is in the village though;
He will not see me stopping here,
To watch his woods fill up with snow.

My little horse must think it queer,
To stop without a farmhouse near,
Between the woods and frozen lake,
The darkest evening of the year.

He gives his harness bells a shake,
To ask if there is some mistake.
The only other sound's the sweep
Of easy wind and downy flake.

The woods are lovely, dark and deep,
But I have promises to keep,
And miles to go before I sleep,
And miles to go before I sleep.

                              Robert Frost

Ferry Me Across the Water
'Ferry me across the water,
        Do, boatman, do.'
'If you've a penny in your purse,
        I'll ferry you.'

'I have a penny in my purse,
        And my eyes are blue;
So ferry me across the water,
        Do, boatman, do!'

'Step into my ferryboat,
        Be they black or blue,
And for the penny in your purse
        I'll ferry you.'

                         Christina Rossetti

Windy Nights
Whenever the moon and stars are set,
        Whenever the wind is high,
All night long in the dark and wet,
        A man goes riding by.
Late in the night when the fires are out,
Why does he gallop and gallop about?

Whenever the trees are crying aloud,
    And ships are tossed at sea,
By, on the highway, low and loud,
    By at the gallop goes he.
By at the gallop he goes and then
By he comes back at the gallop again.
                Robert Louis Stevenson

North-Easter
I love the north-easter
When it whips up the sea
And the kite on its long string
Struggles to be free.

It's blown away the gulls,
It's rattling up a gale –
Look, the yacht heels right over!
A wave grabs the sail!

A thunder-cloud above
Breaks, mumbling and grumbling;
Crowds melt away when
The rain comes tumbling.

I love it, all the wildness
I can watch from our hut,
For I'm warm and bone-dry and
The windows are shut.

'What a chance,' cry the children
'To bathe in wind and rain!'
And they seize me by the hands and
Drag me out again.
                Ian Serraillier

Please to Remember
Here am I
A poor old Guy,
Legs in a bonfire
Head in the sky.

Shoeless my toes,
Wild stars behind,
Smoke in my nose,
And my eye – peeps blind.

Old hat, old straw –
In this disgrace,
While the wild fire gleams
On a mask for face.

Ay, all I am made of
Only trash is;
And soon – soon,
Will be dust and ashes.
                Walter de la Mare

Roadways
One road leads to London,
        One road runs to Wales,
My road leads me seawards
        To the white dipping sails.

One road leads to the river,
        As it goes singing slow;
My road leads to shipping,
        Where the bronzed sailors go.

Leads me, lures me, calls me
        To salt, green, tossing sea;
A road without earth's road-dust
        Is the right road for me.

A wet road, heaving, shining,
        And wild with seagulls' cries,
A mad salt sea-wind blowing
        The salt spray in my eyes.

My road calls me, lures me
        West, east, south, and north;
Most roads lead men homewards,
        My road leads me forth.

To add more miles to the tally
        Of grey miles left behind,
In quest of that one beauty
        God put me here to find.
                John Masefield

Appendix 1: Sources of rhymes and poems

Speech rhymes

Clocks and Watches; Gaffer Gilpin; Washing Day; What's the Weather *Speech Rhymes* edited by Clive Sansom: A. and C. Black

Sweeping *Acting Rhymes* edited by Clive Sansom: A. and C. Black

A hippity hippity hop; Criss-Cross; Dilly-dally; Sing Sing *Speech Training Rhymes and Jingles* by Hilda Haig-Brown and Zillah Walthew: Oxford University Press

Donkey; Drummer Boys; Feathers; Snow; The Butcher's Shop *Junior Rhymes and Jingles* by Kathleen Rich: Samuel French

Splish-Splosh; The Grumpy Grandfather; The Two Rabbits; The Woodman; Windy Nights *The Play Way of Speech Training* by Rodney Bennett: Evans Brothers

Handy Spandy; Higgledy Piggledy; Just like me *The Merry-go-round* rhymes and poems chosen by James Reeves: Puffin

Kan-Kan-Kangaroo *Speech and Communication in the Primary School* by Clive Sansom: A. and C. Black

Feet *Come Follow Me: Poems for the Young*: Evans Brothers

Uncle Vic *Sounds and Rhythm*, Book 1, by Mavis Hampson: Ginn

A Blanket; Bridges; My Glove; Slippers; What a Clatter *Sounds and Rhythm*, Book 3, by Mavis Hampson: Ginn

Rhythm rhymes

Marching; Moppety-Moppit; Rowing *Speech Rhymes* edited by Clive Sansom: A. and C. Black

Jumping; Rush Hour; Swinging *We Play and Grow* by Maisie Cobby: Pitman

Galloping *Rhymes for Speech and Action* by Dorothy Hickman: University of London Press

Look Out! *Songs and Marching Tunes for Children* by Paul Edmonds: Pitman

Skipping; Walking *Rhythm Rhymes* edited by Ruth Sansom: A. and
C. Black

Poems
'Ferry Me Across the Water' by Christina Rossetti *The Merry
Minstrel: an Anthology of Verse for Children*: Blackie
'Here Comes the Band' *We Play and Grow* by Maisie Cobby: Pitman
'Isn't it Cold' *Adventures into Poetry for the Primary School* Intro-
ductory Book: Macmillan
'Mick' *Complete Poems for Children* by James Reeves: Heinemann
'North-Easter' by Ian Serraillier *Happily Ever After*: Oxford
University Press
'Roadways' *The Collected Poems of John Masefield*: Heinemann
'Snowflakes'; 'Bonfire Night' *Skipping Susan*: Evans Brothers
'Stopping by Woods on a Snowy Evening' by Robert Frost *The
Poetry of Robert Frost*: Jonathan Cape
'The Cats Have Come to Tea' by Kate Greenaway *A Child's Book of
Poems*: Collins
'The Goblins' *Come Follow Me: Poems for the Young*: Evans Brothers
'The Huntsmen'; 'Please to Remember' by Walter de la Mare *Secret
Laughter*: Puffin
'The Little Piggies' by Thomas Hood; 'The Snare' by James
Stephens *The Book of a Thousand Poems*: Evans Brothers
'Train Talk' *Poems for Movement*: Evans Brothers
'Windy Nights' by Robert Louis Stevenson *A Child's Garden of
Verses*: Collins

Appendix 2:
Regional Arts Associations

Teachers who wish to know about theatres in their area offering programmes suitable for young children, or about Theatre-in-Education groups which perform in schools, may find it helpful to contact their Regional Arts Association for information about these. A list of the associations is given below.

Eastern Arts Association, 30 Station Road, Cambridge CB1 2JG (Tel: 0223 67707)
Bedfordshire, Cambridgeshire, Essex, Hertfordshire, Norfolk and Suffolk

East Midlands Arts Association, 1 Frederick Street, Loughborough, Leicestershire LE11 3BH (Tel: 0509 67136)
Derbyshire (excluding High Peak District), Leicestershire, Northamptonshire, Nottinghamshire, Milton Keynes District of Buckinghamshire

Greater London Arts Association, 25/31 Tavistock Place, London WC1H 9SF (Tel: 01-387 9541/5)
The area of the thirty-two London Boroughs and the City of London

Lincolnshire and Humberside Arts, Beaumont Lodge, Beaumont Fee, Lincoln LN1 1UN (Tel: 0522 33555)
Lincolnshire and Humberside
North Humberside Area Office, above The White Rabbit Bookshop, 47 North Bar Within, Beverley, North Humberside
Regional Crafts Centre, Jews Court, Steep Hill, Lincoln LN1 (Tel: 0522 33247)

Merseyside Arts Association, Bluecoat Chambers, School Lane, Liverpool L1 3BX (Tel: 051–709 0671/2/3)
Metropolitan County of Merseyside, District of West Lancashire, Ellesmere Port and Halton Districts of Cheshire
Merseyside Arts Shop (Tel: 051–708 7592 – Box Office; 051–708 7576 – Whats On)

Northern Arts, 31 New Bridge Street, Newcastle-upon-Tyne NE1 8JY (Tel: 0632 610446)
Cleveland, Cumbria, Durham, Northumberland, Metropolitan County of Tyne and Wear

North West Arts, 52 King Street, Manchester M2 4LY (Tel: 061–833 9471)
Greater Manchester, High Peak District of Derbyshire, Lancashire (except District of West Lancashire), Cheshire (except Ellesmere Port and Halton Districts)

Southern Arts Association, 19 Southgate Street, Winchester SO23 7EB (Tel: 0962 69422)
Berkshire, Hampshire, Isle of Wight, Oxfordshire, West Sussex, Wiltshire, Districts of Bournemouth, Christchurch and Poole

South East Arts Association, 58 London Road, Southborough, Tunbridge Wells, Kent TN4 0PR (Tel: 0892 38743)
Kent, Surrey and East Sussex

South West Arts, 23 Southernhay East, Exeter, Devon EX1 1QL (Tel: 0392 70338)
Avon, Cornwall, Devon, Dorset (except Districts of Bournemouth, Christchurch and Poole), Gloucestershire, Somerset
Bristol Area Office, 15 Cranbrook Road, Redland, Bristol (Tel: 0272 49340)

West Midlands Arts, Lloyds Bank Chambers, Market Street, Stafford ST16 2AP (Tel: 0785 2788)
County of Hereford and Worcester, Metropolitan County of West Midlands, Shropshire, Staffordshire, Warwickshire
Birmingham Arts Shop, City Arcade, Birmingham B2 4TX (Tel: 021–643 6281)

Yorkshire Arts Association, Glyde House, Glydegate, Bradford, Yorkshire BD5 0BQ (Tel: 0274 23051)
North Yorkshire, South Yorkshire, West Yorkshire

Wales

North Wales Association for the Arts, 10 Wellfield House, Bangor, Gwynedd LL57 1ER (Tel: 0248 53248)
Clwyd, Gwynedd and District of Montgomery in the County of Powys

South East Wales Arts Association, Victoria Street, Cwmbran, Gwent NP4 3JP (Tel: 063-33 67530)
South Glamorgan, Mid-Glamorgan, Gwent, Districts of Radnor and Brecknock in the County of Powys and the City of Cardiff

West Wales Association for the Arts, Dark Gate, Red Street, Carmarthen, Dyfed (Tel: 0267 4248)
Dyfed, West Glamorgan

Other useful addresses

Mid Pennine Association for the Arts, 20 Hammerton Street, Burnley, Lancashire BB11 1NA (Tel: 0282 29513)
North East Lancashire and Yorkshire Border (MPAA is an autonomous area arts association in receipt of grant aid from North West Arts and local authorities.)

Fylde Arts Association, 70 Cookson Street, Blackpool FY1 3DA (Tel: 0253 22130)
Blackpool, Districts of Fylde and Wyre (FAA is an autonomous area arts association in receipt of grant aid from North West Arts and local authorities.)

Scottish Arts Council, 19 Charlotte Square, Edinburgh EH2 4DF (Tel: 031-226 6051)
(The Scottish Arts Council is an autonomous 'committee' of the Arts Council of Great Britain responsible for Scotland.)

Welsh Arts Council, Holst House, Museum Place, Cardiff CF1 3NX (Tel: 0222 394711)
(The Welsh Arts Council is an autonomous 'committee' of the Arts Council of Great Britain responsible for Wales.)

Select Bibliography

ADVISORY COUNCIL ON EDUCATION IN SCOTLAND (1965) *Primary Education* HMSO

ALINGTON, A. F. (1961) *Drama and Education* Blackwell

BRUFORD, R. (1966) *Teaching Mime* Methuen

BURNISTON, C. and BELL, J. (1972) *Into the Life of Things: an exploration of language through verbal dynamics* English Speaking Board

CHAPMAN, E. (1971) *Marmaduke is in a Jam* in *Tell Me Another Story* Puffin

COBBY, M. (1967) *We Play and Grow* Pitman

DODDING, J. (1972) *Mime One* Litho Arts

GILBERT, J. (1975) *Musical Activities with Young Children* Ward Lock Educational

GOODRIDGE, J. (1970) *Drama in the Primary School* Heinemann

HERRMANN, F. and HIM, G. (1964) *The Giant Alexander* Methuen

HEWETT, A. (1966) *Mrs Mopple's Washing Line* Bodley Head

JACKSON, B. and B. (1971) *Models from Junk* Evans Brothers

LEWIS, N. (1975) *Fantasy Books for Children* National Book League

McCREA, L. (1959) *Stories to Play in the Infant School* Oxford University Press

McCULLAGH, S. K. (1966) *The Old Man and the Wind* Hart-Davis Educational

McCULLAGH, S. K. (1966) *Billy Blue Hat and the Duck Pond* Hart-Davis Educational

MELLOR, E. (1953) *Education through Experience in the Infant School* Blackwell

MOREY, S. (1965) *The Old Man and the Turnip* Collins

MORGAN, D. L. (1966) *Living Speech in the Primary School* Longman

ROSS, L. (1973) *Finger Puppets* World's Work

SANSOM, C. (1965) *Speech and Communication in the Primary School* A. and C. Black

SIMPSON, D. and ALDERSON, D. M. (1968) *Creative Play in the Infant School* Pitman

THOMPSON, D. (1973) *Poetry for Children* National Book League

TURSKA, K. (1975) *The Magician of Cracow* Hamish Hamilton Children's Books

WARD, W. (1957 2nd ed) *Playmaking with Children* Appleton-Century-Crofts

WAY, B. (1967) *Development through Drama* Longman

WILDE, O. (1970 ed) *The Happy Prince and Other Stories* Puffin

A selection of poetry and rhyme books

ALDERSON, B. and OXENBURY, H. (1974) *Cakes and Custard* Heinemann

BAYLEY, N. (1975) (Ed) *Nicola Bayley's Book of Nursery Rhymes* Cape

BLEGVAD, L. and E. (1974) *Mittens for Kittens* Hamish Hamilton

BLEGVAD, L. and E. (1975) *Hark, Hark, The Dogs Do Bark* Hamish Hamilton

BLISHEN, E. (1963) (Ed) *Oxford Book of Poetry For Children* Oxford University Press

BROWN, B. C. (1973) *Jonathan Bing* World's Work

CLARK, L. (1974) *Four Seasons* Dobson Books

CLARK, L. (1975) *Collected Poems and Verses for Children* Dobson Books

CUNLIFFE, J. (1971) *Riddles and Rhymes and Rigmaroles* Deutsch

DODD, L. (1976) *The Nickle Nackle Tree* Hamish Hamilton

JEFFERS, S. (1974) *Three Jovial Huntsmen* Hamish Hamilton

LAWRENCE, J. (1976) *Tongue Twisters* Hamish Hamilton

LEAR, E. and DOMANSKA, J. (1974) *Whizz!* Hamish Hamilton

LODGE, B. (1975) *The Grand Old Duke of York* Bodley Head

PRELUTSKY, J. (1975) *Circus* Hamish Hamilton

RASMUSSEN, H. (1973) *Hocus Pocus* Angus and Robertson

REEVES, J. (1967) (Ed) *The Merry-go-round* Puffin

TATE, C. (1971) *Rhymes and Ballads of London* Blackie

THOMPSON, B. (1971) *Lollipops* Longman Young Books

WATSON, C. (1972) *Father Fox's Penny Rhymes* Macmillan

Fifty books for source material

Those marked with an asterisk are noted for their illustrative quality.

*ARTHUR, F. and ROWE, B. (1975) *Captain Rocco Rides to Sheffield* Chatto

BAMBERGER, R. (1971) *My First Big Story Book* Puffin

BERG, L. (1966) *Folk Tales* Hodder and Stoughton Children's Books

BINGLEY, M. (1971) (Ed) *Let's Have A Story* Evans Brothers

*BREINBURG, P. and LLOYD, E. (1974) *Doctor Sean* Bodley Head

CARROLL, L. (1954) *Alice's Adventures in Wonderland* Dent

CLARKE, M. (1965) *First Folk Tales* Hart-Davis

COLLODI, C. (1951) *Pinocchio* Dent

COLWELL, E. (1969) *Time for a Story* Puffin

COLWELL, E. (1971) *Tell me a Story* Puffin

CORRIS, S. and S. (1964) *Stories for Seven Year Olds* Faber

CORRIS, S. and S. (1967) *Stories for Six Year Olds* Faber

CORRIS, S. and S. (1973) *Stories for Five Year Olds* Faber

*COUDRILLE, J. (1975) *Farmer Fisher* G. Wizzard Publications

*CUNLIFFE, J. and HICKSON, J. (1974) *Farmer Barnes and the Snow Picnic* Deutsch

*DONNISON, R. and P. (1975) *Henderson The Supermarket Cat* Sidgwick and Jackson

*FRANCIS, F. (1973) *Natasha's New Doll* (Picture Lion) Collins

*FRENCH, F. (1975) *Aio The Rainmaker* Oxford University Press

GOBLE, P. and D. (1974) *The Friendly Wolf* Macmillan

GOODALL, J. S. (1975) *Creepy Castle* Macmillan

*GRAHAM, M. B. (1974) *Benjy's Dog House* Bodley Head

*GRIMM, J. L. and W. K. (1975) *Thorn Rose* Faber

HALEY, G. E. (1976) *The Post Office Cat* Bodley Head

HOGROGIAN, N. (1974) *Billy Goat and His Well-fed Friends* World's Work

HUGHES, P. (1975) *The Emperor's Oblong Pancake* Abelard-Schuman

*HUTCHINS, P. (1974) *The Wind Blew* Bodley Head

ICHIKAWA, S. (1975) *A Child's Book of Seasons* Heinemann

KEEPING, C. (1966) *Shaun and the Cart-horse* Oxford University Press

*KEEPING, C. (1974) *The Railway Passage* Oxford University Press

LOBEL, A. (1973) *Mouse Tales* World's Work

MCKEE, D. (1972) *The Magician Who Lost His Magic* Pan Books

MCKEE, D. (1974) *The Magician and the Sorcerer* Abelard-Schuman

*MAHY, M. and WILLIAMS, J. (1974) *The Witch in the Cherry Tree* Dent

MAHY, M. (1976) *Leaf Magic* Dent

MILNE, A. A. (1973) *Winnie the Pooh* Methuen Children's Books

MILNE, A. A. (1974) *House at Pooh Corner* Methuen Children's Books

POTTER, B. (1976) *The Tale of Peter Rabbit* Frederick Warne

POTTER, B. (1976) *The Tailor of Gloucester* Frederick Warne
POWER, R. (1967) *Ten Minute Tales* Evans Brothers
POWER, R. (1969) *Seven Minute Tales* Evans Brothers
*PRELUTSKY, J. and LOBEL, A. (1975) *The Terrible Tiger* Bodley Head
PYLE, H. (1965) *The Wonder Clock* Dover Publications
ROBERTON, J. E. (1961) *Hans Andersen Fairy Tales* Blackie
ROCKWELL, A. (1975) *The Three Bears and Fifteen Other Stories* Hamish Hamilton
*ROSE, E. and G. (1974) *Wolf! Wolf!* Faber
*SANSOM, W. and ABRAHAMS, H. (1974) *Skimpy* Deutsch
SHARMAT, M. and W. (1974) *Nate the Great* World's Work
STEIG, W. (1975) *The Real Thief* Hamish Hamilton
*STUBBS, J. (1975) *The Tree House* Deutsch
TOMALIN, B. (1975) *A Green Wishbone* Faber

Index